Eyewitness
CHINA

Calligraphy
writing set

男人
女人

Road toll receipt,
Chengdu

Bus ticket,
Beijing

Bus ticket,
Nanjing

Kung fu
students

Bamboo

Moon cakes

Eyewitness
CHINA

Written by
POPPY SEBAG-MONTEFIORE

Consultant
ZHOU XUN

Children
walking to
school

Chopsticks, used at every dinner table in China

Simplified Chinese character for "cloud"

Traditional Chinese character for "cloud"

LONDON, NEW YORK, MELBOURNE, MUNICH, AND DELHI

Project editor Ben Hoare
Senior art editor David Ball
Managing editor Camilla Hallinan
Managing art editor Martin Wilson
Publishing manager Sunita Gahir
Category publisher Andrea Pinnington
Picture researchers Louise Thomas, Claire Bowers
Production controller Angela Graef
Jacket designer Andy Smith

DK DELHI
Head of publishing Aparna Sharma
Senior designer Romi Chakraborty
Designer Mini Dhawan
DTP designer Govind Mittal

First published in the United States in 2007
by DK Publishing, 375 Hudson Street, New York, New York 10014

12 13 10 9 8 7 6 5 4
013 – ED493 – Jul/2007

DK books are available at special discounts when purchased in bulk for sales promotions, premiums, fundraising, or educational use. For details, contact: DK Publishing Special Markets 375 Hudson Street, New York, New York 10014 SpecialSales@dk.com

A catalog record for this book is available from the Library of Congress.

ISBN: 978-0-7566-2976-2 (HC); 978-0-7566-2975-5 (Library Binding)

Color reproduction by Colourscan, Singapore
Printed and bound in China by HUNG HING Printing Co. Ltd

A selection of Chinese-language media published in China and overseas

Silk dress from a fashion show in Hong Kong

Yin Yang symbol

Discover more at
www.dk.com

Contents

Laughing Buddha statue, a symbol of
wealth and fertility in China

The day begins

As MORNING COMES, PEOPLE in China spend their first few hours awake in many different ways. Older people often exercise outdoors with their friends and neighbors, before visiting the early market for a snack and to buy fresh food for the rest of the day. The market vendors boil eggs in tea and sell bread rolls, soy milk, and buns filled with sweet beans. Younger people may just be getting up when their parents return with breakfast. The journey to work or school can involve struggling along traffic-choked city streets or a walk down quiet country lanes, but either way it may be a long trip. People staying at home tell their relatives to "go slowly"—the Chinese for "goodbye."

RUSH HOUR IN THE CITY
Commuters cycle to work quite slowly, but if it begins to rain they pick up the pace and the whole city changes rhythm. Wide cycle paths run alongside major roads, and since driving through bustling cities is stressful, cycling is the best way to travel in the morning rush.

PARK LIFE
In the morning China's parks, squares, and gardens buzz and hum as groups of people join in with all kinds of cultural activities and physical exercise. Here, a group of elderly Hong Kong residents are practicing Tai Chi—a gentle exercise that features lots of stretching and deep, relaxed breathing. Some people sing opera outdoors, or take their pet birds for a stroll in a wooden cage.

Large fan for making elegant, sweeping movements

GOING TO SCHOOL
These city children are making the short walk to their nearby primary school. Now more parents own cars and so can give their children a ride. But for many children in the countryside, the walk to school may take several hours across rough or mountainous terrain. The first activity at school, before classes start, is morning exercises in the playground.

6

> *"Work begins with sunrise, rest begins with sundown. Carefree, I wander between the heavens and the Earth."*

ZHUANG ZHOU
Philosopher, 4th century BCE

FAN DANCERS
It is early morning in Shanghai, and these local people have gathered on a walkway beside the river to dance with large, colorful fans. They might dance to live music or bring a cassette player and a large speaker to set the beat. One member of the group leads the dancing, and by the end everyone feels energized. Fan dancing has a long history in China, and the need to revive the body and mind each morning is an important custom.

EATING ON THE MOVE
Stalls selling breakfast snacks pop up all over China's towns and cities from 5:30 a.m. until around 9 a.m. At this stall, people are buying fried dough twists and pancakes filled with pork, mutton, or eggs with green vegetables.

RURAL BREAKFAST
For many villagers breakfast is a simple meal, often of rice or noodles. It is sometimes eaten in a hurry while standing up, using chopsticks or just fingers. But breakfast is still an important occasion when people greet each other with best wishes for the day ahead.

GATHERING FIREWOOD
Work begins very early in the countryside—usually at dawn as soon as it is light. Before making breakfast, people may go out to gather wood to heat the kitchen stove. Another essential morning chore is to fetch food and water for their animals.

Diverse land

CHINA IS A COLOSSAL COUNTRY with a fantastic variety of landscapes, wildlife, peoples, and customs. It is the most populous nation on Earth— 1.3 billion people live here, or one in five of all humans alive today. Ninety percent of China's population take the ethnic identity "Han," but there are 55 other ethnic groups in China, each with its own languages, and traditions. Vast areas of the north and west are a barren wilderness, but the crowded east coast is lined with megacities, ports, and booming industrial zones. In the southeast are jungles and hot tropical lowlands. To the southwest lies the Plateau of Tibet, an enormous region of rock and ice that meets the foothills of the Himalayan mountains. Two mighty rivers—the Yangtze and the Yellow River—cut across China to the ocean and provide a vital transport link.

FEEDING THE NATION
This woman from the Dai ethnic group is carrying baskets of rice seedlings to plant in Yunnan province, south China. Rice was probably first grown in China in around 8500 BCE and it is still the main staple food. Rice is so important to Chinese life that one of the most common greetings is *Chi fan le ma?*, which means "Have you eaten rice yet today?"

WHERE IN THE WORLD
China covers around 3.7 million square miles (9.6 million km²) of land in central and eastern Asia and is the world's fourth largest country. Its long coastline meets the East China Sea and the South China Sea, which form part of the Pacific Ocean.

THE HIMALAYAS
Many peaks in this range, known as the "Roof of the World," soar nearly 20,000 ft (6,000 m) above sea level. Here at Mount Everest base camp in Tibet is where expeditions set off to climb the tallest mountain of them all, which rises to 29,029 ft (8,850 m). Tibetans call it *Chomolungma* or "Goddess Mother of the World."

PEOPLE OF TIBET
There are 4.6 million Tibetans in China—half in Tibet and the rest in the nearby Chinese provinces of Qinghai, Gansu, Sichuan, and Yunnan. China took control of Tibet in September 1951.

NORTHERN DESERT
Almost one-fifth of China's land is
desert. The largest deserts are in the northwest, where
sand dunes and rocky plains stretch in all directions.
Bactrian camels are among the few animals that can
survive this tough environment. The
local Uyghur people use camels
for transport and burn their
dung as fuel.

MODERN METROPOLIS
Hong Kong is a small island off the
coast of southeast China. At night
its bright neon glow and glittering
skyscrapers are one of China's most
famous views. Away from the high-
rise city center, three-quarters of
Hong Kong is forest and mountains.

MIAO PEOPLE
South China is home to
around nine million Miao
people. There are many
different Miao communities, such
as the *Hmong*, and each dresses
differently and wears distinct hair
styles and silverwork. Other
groups of Miao people live in
Vietnam, Laos, and Cambodia.

WINDSWEPT GRASSLAND
The treeless hills and plains of northeast China have an extremely harsh
climate, with bitterly cold winters and
hot, dry summers. Few people inhabit
this remote but beautiful land. Most
are Mongolian nomads, who herd
cattle, sheep, and goats on horseback.

NATURAL BEAUTY
The stunning scenery of the Li River in Guangxi province has
inspired many of China's greatest writers and artists. The river
loops between steep-sided crags draped with lush vegetation, and
fertile farmland covers the valley floor. Each peak is given a name
that describes its shape, such as Elephant Trunk Hill.

A long history

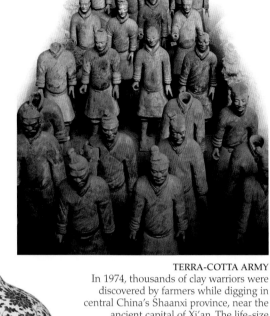

THE EARLIEST HUMAN remains found in China date back 600,000 years and for the last 4,000 years it has been the oldest continuous civilization on Earth. People first settled on the fertile banks of the Yellow River, known as China's "mother river." They developed tools to cultivate crops, but their lords were often at war. The first great ruling dynasty in China was the Shang (c. 1650–1027 BCE). Yet China's many warring kingdoms were not united as a single empire until 221 BCE. This event marked the birth of the Qin Dynasty (221–207 BCE), which created a standard script and currency to strengthen its rule. The Han Dynasty (207 BCE–220 CE) built a powerful civil service to run the empire. Over the next 2,000 years China's imperial system was shaken by dynastic power struggles and foreign conquest, but it lasted to 1912.

BRONZE AGE
This bronze dagger was cast during the Shang Dynasty when skillful metalworkers created some of the finest bronze objects ever made, including knives, spears, ax heads, and sacrificial vessels. Fragments of ancient Chinese script carved on bone have survived

TERRA-COTTA ARMY
In 1974, thousands of clay warriors were discovered by farmers while digging in central China's Shaanxi province, near the ancient capital of Xi'an. The life-size soldiers, some with horses, have guarded the underground tomb of China's first emperor, Qin Shi Huang, since 209 BCE. When the model army was unearthed it was brightly painted, but the pigments faded after exposure to air. Today, the site is one of China's top tourist attractions.

Blue comes from cobalt oxide

PORCELAIN MASTERPIECES
Arts and crafts were mass-produced during the Ming Dynasty (1368–1644). Many beautiful Ming vases, often with blue and white decoration, were exported and the best examples now fetch over 10 million dollars. Under the Ming emperors, the capital moved to Beijing and Chinese power reached its peak.

Kublai Khan

Kublai Khan's hunting party, painted on silk

MONGOL WARRIOR
In the 13th century China was conquered by the Mongols from the north, and the warrior emperor Kublai Khan controlled a vast empire stretching from Europe across Asia. Khan founded China's Yuan Dynasty, which ruled from 1279 to 1368.

DANGEROUS VICE

Opium, an addictive drug derived from poppies, was widely smoked in China during the Qing Dynasty. People usually put a mixture of opium and tobacco in long pipes and smoked it while drinking tea. Most of the opium came from India and was supplied by Britain, which fought two wars with China in the 19th century when China tried to ban opium imports.

Carved bamboo stem

Antique opium pipe, or "smoking pistol"

Pu Yi as emperor of Japanese Manchuria, c. 1940

THE LAST EMPEROR

Pu Yi began his extraordinary life as a revered child emperor. He was the last emperor of the Qing Dynasty, which seized control of China in 1644. Pu Yi inherited the throne in 1908 when still a baby, but four years later China became a republic and Pu Yi resigned. China's age of imperial rule was over. During the 1930s Japan occupied Manchuria in northeast China and installed Pu Yi as "emperor." After Japan's defeat in 1945, Pu Yi was imprisoned by the Communist Party, but later released to lead a quiet life as an ordinary citizen.

Watchtowers at regular intervals

GREAT WALL OF CHINA

During the 3rd century BCE the Qin emperors started to build a huge stone wall to stop goods from being smuggled out of China. Later dynasties, particularly the Ming emperors, also built walls in the north to protect against raiding nomadic tribes from Mongolia, and the last stones were laid in the 17th century. The fortification snakes for 1,500 miles (2,414 km) from the western desert to the ocean, and is the world's largest human structure.

War and revolution

After the end of imperial rule in 1912, China was torn apart by bitter conflicts and violent political upheavals. The new republic was weak and many groups struggled for power, including warlords, the Chinese Communist Party, and the Chinese Nationalist Party, or Kuomintang (KMT). In 1937, these groups united to fight China's greatest enemy, Japan, but after their victory in 1945, civil war erupted again in China. Eventually, Communist troops crushed the Nationalist resistance, whose leaders fled overseas to Taiwan to set up a rival government. In 1949, Mao Zedong established the People's Republic of China on the Chinese mainland, starting a revolution that lasted over 25 years. He banned religion, outlawed private wealth, and attacked old methods of farming, business, and education. China emerged as a new kind of state based partly on Communism and partly on rule by fear.

ATTACK ON NANJING
Japan's aircraft bomb Nanjing in 1937 during the Chinese-Japanese war of 1937–1945. After the city fell, Japanese troops looted it and killed thousands of Chinese civilians. But China rebuilt its army and, with support from the US, fought back to win the war in the end.

REVOLUTIONARY LEADER
Mao Zedong (also known as Mao Tse-Tung) turned China upside down to achieve his Communist vision. He was a brutal leader, and in 1958–1961 at least 30 million people died of famine caused by his policies. But Chinese are taught to give Mao credit for trying to help ordinary workers and making China strong.

Book is small enough to fit in a shirt pocket

THE LITTLE RED BOOK
Quotations from Chairman Mao's writings and speeches were published in 1964 in a pocket volume known as the *Little Red Book*. They sum up Mao's sayings and explain how to be a good citizen of Communist China. During the Cultural Revolution, people were told to carry the book at all times and to study Mao's words at school and work. Around 900 million copies of the *Little Red Book* were printed—more than any other book in the world except for the Bible.

CULTURAL REVOLUTION
From 1965 until Mao's death in 1976, China's Communist Party waged a vicious battle against old ways of life. University teachers, writers, business owners, government officials, and politicians who were seen to be against the revolution were punished as traitors. Many students like these joined a movement called the Red Guard. Mobs of Red Guards scoured China to round up Mao's enemies.

"A revolution is not a dinner party or writing an essay… it is an act of violence… by which one class overthrows another."

MAO ZEDONG
March 1927

Mao pictured in casual clothes, as one of the people

PEOPLE'S COMMUNES
Mao confiscated land from private landlords and divided it among the people. He organized the countryside into communes, each made up of a few thousand families. A commune shared everything, from the farmland to the dining halls, schoolhouse, and even furniture. Nothing belonged to the individual. This imaginary scene shows contented workers welcoming Mao to their commune, but in reality his disastrous policy was a tragedy for China. Harvests collapsed, millions starved, and normal society broke down.

THE BIRTH OF MODERN CHINA

Deng Xiaoping, who appears on this billboard poster, was the main Communist leader in China from the late 1970s until the early 1990s. He reversed many of Mao's policies and encouraged people to set up their own businesses and trade with each other. Under Deng, China became one of the world's fastest growing economies.

THE UNKNOWN REBEL

A lone protestor bravely halts Chinese government tanks on a street in Beijing in June 1989. This man was part of a student movement that had been demanding political and economic changes for weeks. Throughout April and May 1989, big crowds of protestors gathered on Tian'an Men Square in central Beijing. They refused to leave, and on June 4 the army was ordered to open fire. Hundreds of people were killed and thousands injured. To this day, information about the events of 1989 is restricted in the Chinese media.

HONG KONG HANDOVER

China's leaders regained control of Hong Kong at this ceremony on June 30, 1997, after more than 150 years of British rule in the territory. Hong Kong had been seized by British forces in 1840, when the Chinese empire was in decline and surrounded by enemies. Later, Chinese officials signed a treaty to let Britain run Hong Kong until 1997. Since the handover, it has been a semi-independent region of China, with a separate legal system and economy.

Sun

Character for "bright"

Moon

WRITING SYSTEM
Chinese script uses symbols instead of the letters of an alphabet. Some of these characters are made up of separate elements added together. For example, the character for "bright" (above) combines the symbols for two bright things—"Moon" and "Sun."

Speaking Chinese

CHINESE IS LIKE A FAMILY OF thousands of dialects and accents, and it is spoken by more people than any other language. Mandarin is China's national language, taught in schools across the country and used on the television and radio. But in each province and even in different towns and villages people speak their own local dialect. Some of these are so distinct that many people around the country cannot understand each other unless they use Mandarin. Chinese characters come from one of the world's oldest writing systems. A Chinese dictionary is home to up to 56,000 characters, and people need to learn around 6,000 to read a good book.

MAO'S SCRIPT
The title of the *People's Daily* newspaper uses a typeface based on Chairman Mao's own handwriting. His calligraphy was displayed more widely than that of any other Chinese leader. With practice, it is said to be possible to interpret the personality and interests of a writer from the style of his or her calligraphy.

Mao's script

CALLIGRAPHER AT WORK
Calligraphy is a style of elaborate, flowing handwriting that requires dedicated practice, created using pens and brushes of different shapes and sizes. It is customary in China to give beautifully written calligraphy as presents, and this master calligrapher is writing lucky characters to sell at his stall. One of the most popular characters is *fu*, meaning "lucky," which many Chinese people paste to the gate of their home.

HONG KONG SIGNS
The tiny island of Hong Kong used to be a colony, and has kept an older style of writing characters—as seen in these neon signs. The islanders speak a dialect called Cantonese, and most only started learning Mandarin after Hong Kong was handed back to China in 1997.

Traditional form   Simplified form

TWO WRITING STYLES
These are the traditional and simplified Chinese characters for "cloud." Chinese characters adapt over time, and in 1964 the government completed a plan to simplify Chinese script. People in Hong Kong, Macau, and Taiwan still use the more traditional characters.

Character for "kebab"

KEBAB PICTOGRAM
The illuminated sign hanging above this street kiosk is the Chinese character *chuan*, which means "kebab." This type of character is called a pictogram because it is a drawing of the word it represents. Around 600 Chinese characters are pictograms.

INKSTONE AND BRUSH
Calligraphers need ink, an inkstone to hold it, a brush, and paper. In China these traditionally are known as the "four treasures of the library." Chinese ink is made of a combination of lampblack (black soot) and glue. It is shaped into solid blocks called ink sticks, then mixed with water in the inkstone before use.

Inkstone

Ink stick

Goat's hair brush

Arabic script

Chinese script

Uyghur script

ONE COUNTRY, MANY LANGUAGES
This dentist's advertisement is written in three languages: Arabic; an old form of Uyghur; and Chinese. It comes from a Muslim part of China, Xinjiang province, where the native population is mostly Uyghur, one of the 55 officially recognized ethnic minority groups in China. Each ethnic group has its own language.

Character for fu ("lucky")

Citizenship

ANYONE BORN IN CHINA to at least one Chinese parent is considered a Chinese national. Here citizenship centers around the idea that everyone in the country is part of one big family or *tongbao*, meaning "common ancestry." Many Chinese talk about their deep love for their motherland.

One of the cultural ideals in China suggests that people should aim to coexist happily with others, and not just seek their own happiness. Often shared desires for social stability can override concerns for individual rights. For example, migrant workers in the cities do not enjoy full rights but cannot afford to complain. Many Chinese say that during the early stages of a modern nation, it is important to develop the economy first, before their children can enjoy greater freedom to do and say what they want. But if people feel their rights as citizens are not being respected, they sometimes stage protests against the state.

CHINESE FLAG
The modern Chinese flag was designed in 1949, soon after the Communist Party came to power. The red background symbolizes the blood of those who died in the civil war and defending China from Japanese invasion. The large yellow star symbolizes the Party leadership, and the four smaller stars represent the four classes of society.

TEAHOUSE DISCUSSION
A teahouse is a popular place for people of all ages to meet and exchange news over cups of tea. These personal networks are often highly reliable and swift ways of passing information between people, especially since it can take a long time to receive information from official institutions.

TIAN'AN MEN SQUARE
Situated at the heart of Beijing, this is the largest square in the world, with enough space to hold a million people. It has been the political center of China since imperial times, and *Tian'an Men* literally means "receiving the mandate from heaven and stabilizing the dynasty." The site used to contain offices of the emperor, but Mao Zedong made it into an open public space.

BUYING SHARES
Every day millions of shares change hands on China's Stock Exchange. Following Deng Xiaoping's economic reforms in 1989, many people began to see making money as a path to greater personal freedom. As people's personal wealth increased, they felt able to make more choices about how they live.

MILITARY MIGHT
The People's Liberation Army (PLA), with its 2.25 million active troops, is the world's largest military force. It consists of an army, navy, air force, and strategic nuclear corps. The PLA stages enormous parades to display the Chinese government's power and its ability to protect China from attack.

CELEBRATING NATIONAL DAY
Hundreds of thousands of people gather on Tian'an Men Square in Beijing on China's National Day (October 1) to mark the anniversary of the founding of the People's Republic of China. Many wave red Chinese flags and there are parades and spectacular firework displays. Everyone in China can take a week-long vacation to celebrate this event and many people from the provinces use the occasion to visit their capital city.

Communist Party slogan

Tibetan women dressed up for a photocall to promote the elections

VILLAGE ELECTIONS
These women from Qinghai province in northwest China are voting for their village leaders. These elections are only local—no one votes for China's national party leaders. Some village elections are carried out fairly and successfully. In others, however, officials sometimes restrict the number of candidates and manipulate the voting system.

PRO-DEMOCRACY PROTEST
Each year on July 1, local people hold a pro-democracy demonstration on the streets of Hong Kong. They are determined to keep the system of democracy and freedom of speech designed by British bureaucrats for the island's self-rule when the UK handed Hong Kong back to China in 1997.

Changing fashions

DURING THE AGE OF EMPERORS, fine robes were a sign of rank and good taste, although ordinary Chinese wore basic clothes made of rough materials. When the Communist Party came to power in China, it swept aside old fashions—everyone from a farmer to the country's leaders had to wear the same clothes. Now people can wear what they like. Most prefer modern, Western-style clothing because old Chinese styles have become expensive, but people of China's ethnic minorities still make their own styles of clothes by hand.

Headdress based on an old design from south China

Robe fastens at the side

IMPERIAL ROBE
This embroidered silk robe was made in the 19th century during the final decades of the Qing Dynasty. Under the emperors, silk was worn only by members of the imperial court and powerful officials, to show their high status.

Dragon motif

Wave border

Luxurious hem in gold thread

Colorful hat with tassel

Heavy silver necklace

COSTUME FROM GUIZHOU
Each ethnic group in China has its own styles of clothing and adornment, such as hats and jewelry. Today, these outfits are usually worn only for festivals and other important occasions, but some people locally wear them every day. In Guizhou province in southwest China, Miao women sew beautiful panels onto their clothes. The finer the design, the better a girl's marriage prospects.

Silk fabric with delicate embroidery

Long sleeves look like exotic feathers

CATWALK FASHION
The glamorous dress shown here was created for a catwalk show in Hong Kong. Shopping for expensive clothes and watching fashion shows are popular among China's growing numbers of rich people. The country's top fashion designers mix Chinese fabrics, patterns, and sewing techniques with Western styles.

SYMBOL OF MODERNITY
Western-style suit jackets have replaced Mao suits as everyday work clothes in China, even on construction sites. The suits are affordable because they are mass-produced in Chinese factories, and are a symbol of the country's new business culture.

Barrow laden with building tools and equipment

Suit jacket worn instead of coveralls

"Now all the young people's clothes are factory-made. They don't want traditional costume."

ANONYMOUS
Female weaver, Yunnan province, 1997

YOUTH CULTURE
Rock and punk are a way of life in China and not just a type of music. Their fans reject mainstream Chinese society and politics, making them unpopular with the government. This underground youth culture is vibrant, rebellious, and quick to adopt new trends.

MAO SUIT
This famous blue uniform is known as the Mao suit and once was worn by most Chinese men and women. Despite its name it was invented not by Mao Zedong, but by Sun Yat-sen, China's first leader when it became a republic in 1911. He wanted to get rid of imperial styles of clothing and modernize the country. Based on a new Japanese fashion, the uniform was designed to be comfortable, simple, and cheap. Today, Mao suits are mostly worn by the elderly.

Matching peaked cap

Button-up jacket made of tough cotton

PRACTICAL CLOTHING
In the countryside most people have little money for clothes. They dress simply in items that will keep them cool in summer and warm in winter. For example, straw hats keep off the sun and rain while working outdoors. Many women put on arm covers like the ones in this photograph, to keep their sleeves clean while they work in the fields or inside factories.

Hutongs and high-rises

CHAI
This Chinese character means "demolition." It is used to mark the walls of *hutongs* to be knocked down to make room for new buildings.

ANCIENT NARROW ALLEYWAYS called *hutongs* once wove through Beijing and still survive in the city's old neighborhoods. They are lined on both sides by the outer walls of one story courtyard homes. Cooking, bathing, pigeon rearing, games of chess, and many other household and social activities take place on the quiet streets outside. Beijing is growing at a massive rate, and since the 1990s lots of *hutongs* have been demolished to make way for wider roads and new high-rise apartment blocks. Some people enjoy the privacy and convenience of a modern apartment, but others regret the loss of their relaxed, communal way of life.

Upper quarters

Ancestral hall at center of building

Circular open roof

Earth outer wall

Communal lower level

ROUNDHOUSE
Many of China's regional housing styles are in use to this day. In Fujian province, the Hakka people have been building circular homes called *tulou* since the 17th century. These have thick walls of rammed earth with no windows low down, originally for defense. The open-plan lower level may be shared by several hundred residents.

TRADITIONAL HOUSES
Located in the shadow of Shanghai's main business district, this old street has a tight-knit community. Today, fewer city dwellers live in a maze of low-rise streets like this, and the new blocks that replace them are neatly arranged on a grid system. Traditional housing is fast disappearing from many cities around China.

CRAMPED LIVING

Several families often live in crowded conditions in the same courtyard home. Each house in Beijing's *hutongs* once belonged to a single family, but in the late 1950s China's Communist regime began to enforce communal living, so people had to divide up the properties.

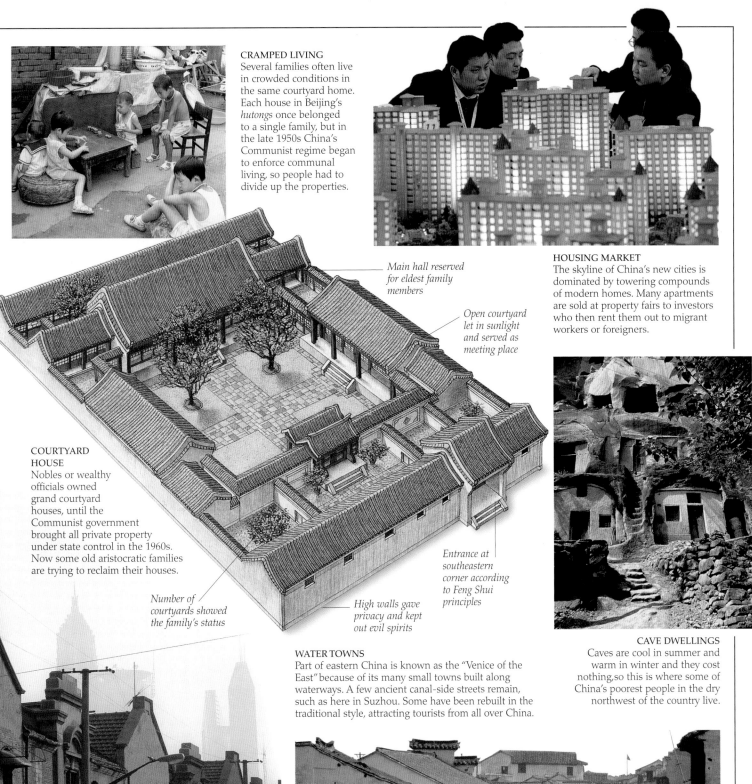

HOUSING MARKET

The skyline of China's new cities is dominated by towering compounds of modern homes. Many apartments are sold at property fairs to investors who then rent them out to migrant workers or foreigners.

Main hall reserved for eldest family members

Open courtyard let in sunlight and served as meeting place

COURTYARD HOUSE

Nobles or wealthy officials owned grand courtyard houses, until the Communist government brought all private property under state control in the 1960s. Now some old aristocratic families are trying to reclaim their houses.

Entrance at southeastern corner according to Feng Shui principles

Number of courtyards showed the family's status

High walls gave privacy and kept out evil spirits

CAVE DWELLINGS

Caves are cool in summer and warm in winter and they cost nothing, so this is where some of China's poorest people in the dry northwest of the country live.

WATER TOWNS

Part of eastern China is known as the "Venice of the East" because of its many small towns built along waterways. A few ancient canal-side streets remain, such as here in Suzhou. Some have been rebuilt in the traditional style, attracting tourists from all over China.

Welcome home

As in most countries, a home in China is above all a sanctuary where people can relax with their families and take refuge from the outside world. But Chinese families live closely together, sometimes sharing rooms or even beds, and many elderly grandparents move in with their children and grandchildren. Finding peace within such crowded conditions is an art that Chinese people think is important. The Chinese are very house-proud and in spring they clean their houses from top to bottom ready for the New Year festival. Cleaning is believed to drive away bad luck and prepare the household for good luck to arrive. Some families give their windows and doors a new coat of red paint, which is considered to be a lucky color. Many homes in China are built and arranged to Feng Shui principles. Feng Shui is a practice that tries to find a harmony between people and their surroundings. It includes mystical ideas and practical advice, such as where to put furniture.

CENTRAL HEATING SYSTEM
Old Chinese farmhouses, especially in north China, may have a bench called a *kang* built into the wall of their main room. This home has two of them on which the whole family sleeps together. In the sturdy brick base is an empty space that traps hot air piped from a stove. The bricks stay warm all night, even if the fire goes out. By day a *kang* functions as a table or sofa and is the heart of the home.

ALL IN ONE ROOM
This couple from Beijing are typical of many young families in Chinese cities. They share a small two-room apartment with their daughter, and everyone has to eat, sleep, get dressed, watch television, and study in the same room. Despite their lack of living space, the parents have secure jobs, so they can give priority to buying things for their child, such as a computer, books, and toys.

Feng Shui chart

FENG SHUI CONSULTANT
When people buy a new home, they may hire a Feng Shui expert to make sure it is in a good location and to help them design its layout. The consultant uses instruments such as a circular chart or *bagua* to measure the flow of "natural energy" around the building.

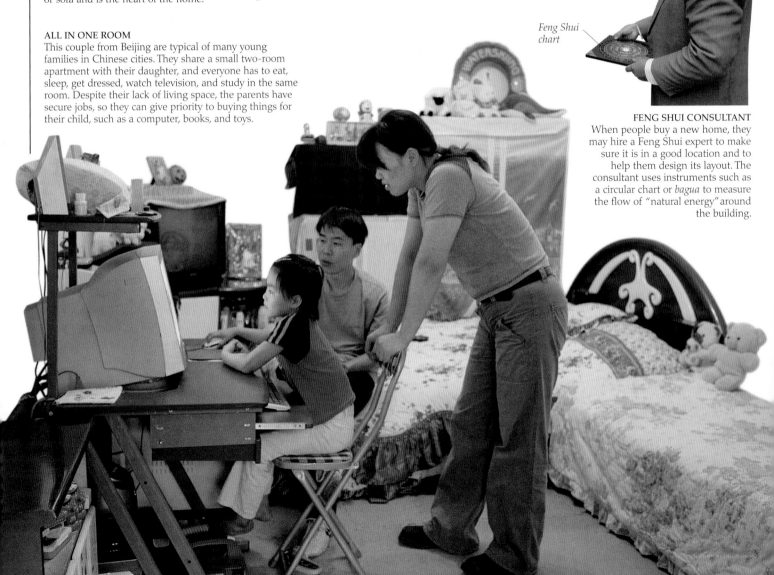

EVENING ENTERTAINMENT

Each night millions of games of Mahjong are played in Chinese homes, especially when friends meet up on the weekend. It is a game of chance and skill for four players, with complex rules similar to the card game Bridge. Mahjong uses small tiles that belong to three suits (Bamboos, Circles, and Characters) and the goal is to build complete sets. There are also special pieces, including Wind, Dragon, and Flower tiles, which help decide the course of play.

Insulated hot water flask

Traditional floral pattern

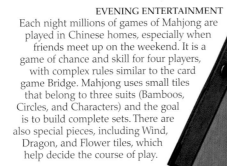

Mahjong tiles are usually made of plastic or marble

REFRESHING DRINKS

Until recently you could find flasks like this in every Chinese home. Families boiled water in a wok on the stove and the flasks kept it warm so that they could enjoy cups of tea or hot water all day. The flasks used to be a sign of modernity and were given as a marriage gift, but now they are being replaced by electric kettles.

COVERING THE FEET

When people enter a Chinese home they always take off their outdoor shoes and put on slippers, flip-flops, or pumps. No one walks around indoors with bare feet. Most homes have tiled or earth floors that are chilly to touch and it is an ancient Chinese belief that if your feet get too cold you will get sick.

Slippers are offered to guests as they arrive

Pekingese dog – a breed native to Beijing (formerly Peking)

MAN'S BEST FRIEND

Pet dogs were banned in China during the Cultural Revolution of the 1960s and 1970s because the Communist Party thought that they were an unnecessary luxury. Today, dogs are highly fashionable again. Families often keep a pet dog for security or companionship, and wealthy people own pedigree breeds as a status symbol.

Doing the dishes is often done in a bowl on the floor

SIMPLE FURNISHINGS

Poor families in China usually own little furniture aside from a few beds, a table, some chairs and stools, and perhaps a wardrobe or cupboard. Their most important possession is likely to be a heavy iron or clay stove that burns wood or coal, which is used for cooking and to heat the home. People crouch on the floor or sit on low stools to cook, clean pots and dishes, and do the laundry. The stools are often beautiful antiques, used for generations.

Roof opens at top for ventilation

Sides may have windows and doors

MOBILE HOMES

Many of China's minority groups have their own types of home. Nomadic Mongolians live in tents called yurts or *gers* (left), made of heavy felt or canvas on a wooden frame. A *ger* is comfortable inside (above), with plenty of space for a big family.

Megacities

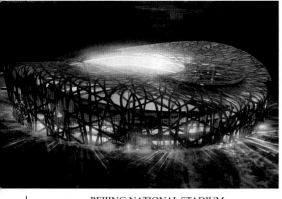

BEIJING NATIONAL STADIUM
This is a computer graphic of the sports stadium for the 2008 Olympic Games in Beijing, which can seat up to 100,000 spectators. Its complex steel structure, which looks like woven twigs, has earned it the nickname of "Bird's Nest." Giant building projects in Chinese cities are a sign of China's increasing wealth in the 21st century.

Chinese cities include some of the fastest growing urban areas on Earth. Shanghai is by far the largest city in China, and the eighth largest in the world, with a population of 14.5 million in 2005. China's next biggest cities are Beijing, Guangzhou, Shenzen, Wuhan, and Hong Kong. Most Chinese still live in the countryside, but this is changing as poor people migrate to cities to find better paid jobs. Half of the country's population will probably be city-dwellers by 2015. The rapid expansion of China's cities causes problems, such as pollution, overcrowding, and shortages of electricity and water.

MODERN SHANGHAI
In this aerial view of Shanghai, a network of busy roads forms a spiral to connect with the Nanpu Bridge, which crosses the Huangpu River at the top left of the photograph. Shanghai is the commercial, financial, and manufacturing center of China. But this metropolis was not a major city until the 1860s, and at one time it was a sleepy fishing village.

URBAN POLLUTION

Life in Chinese cities is often unhealthy because of pollution. The air in many cities is so heavily polluted with vehicle exhaust fumes and smoke from factories that cyclists wear face masks. Water supplies are polluted by factory waste and untreated sewage that flow into rivers and lakes. Cities are trying to clean their environment—for example, by banning older cars with dirtier exhausts.

TRAFFIC CONGESTION

Long, wide avenues slice across China's cities. They used to be empty and quiet, but now they are noisy highways jammed with traffic as more people can afford to buy their own cars. It may take an hour just to travel a few miles.

Meat for sale at a butcher's mobile stall

POVERTY

There were hardly any beggars on China's city streets before the 1980s. Previously, the Communist regime guaranteed people a job and home and it enforced travel restrictions that stopped migration. China does not control its economy so strictly today. Cities are wealthier under the new system, but the poorest are left homeless with little or no state support, and have to beg.

STREET FOOD

Vendors set up stalls on street corners, in alleyways and squares, or under road bridges—wherever there is room. There is always a huge variety of fresh food, snacks, or delicious cooked meals for sale.

BUILDING BOOM

More than 50 cities in China are home to at least a million people. To deal with overcrowding the city planners build upward, because high-rise apartment blocks and offices allow more people to live and work in the same area. The vast building sites create tens of thousands of construction jobs, and many people leave the countryside to work there. Wages are usually low, but the migrant workers earn more than they did before.

New high-rise apartments

Building under construction

Old houses awaiting demolition

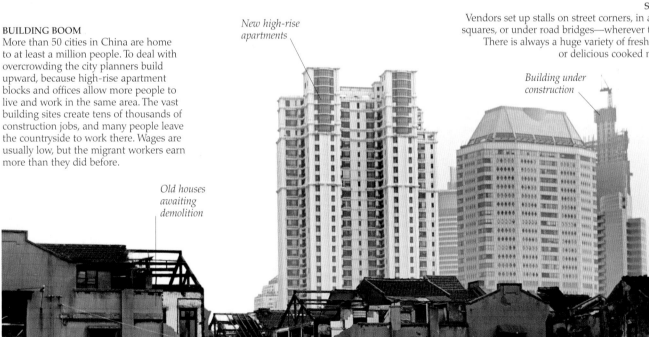

On the move

PEOPLE ARE MOVING AROUND China more than ever before. Until the 1990s it was hard to make long journeys in China because the government restricted where and how often its citizens could travel. Many people spent virtually their entire lives in the same town or village. Today, growing numbers of people in China can afford to travel across the country on buses and the railroad to find work, go to college, or take a vacation. In the cities, millions of commuters are buying cars to replace their bicycles. Air travel—once a dream for most Chinese people—is booming, too. To cope with this demand, China's government plans to build new highways and open several new airports every year.

RIVER TRAFFIC
In China's inland provinces people often take a water taxi to work. Ten percent of the cargo in China is ferried along rivers and canals by boat, especially in remote parts of the center and south.

Road toll receipt

Bus tickets

BIKE PARKING
There are so many bicycles in China's cities that commuters pay to use bike parking lots because there is no sidewalk space. Some cities have banned bicycles from main roads to make more room for traffic, causing severe pollution.

FREEDOM TO TRAVEL
There is a vast railroad and bus network in China, and public transportation is cheap. But during China's old Communist system there were strict controls on cross-country travel. People could not buy a long-distance train ticket or a plane ticket whenever they wanted. They first had to ask permission from their employer, who issued a letter to get a ticket. Permission was also needed to stay in most hotels or to travel abroad. Today, such restrictions have been lifted to help the economy grow.

Driver walks or runs

RICKSHAW
Human rickshaws like this one for tourists are a reminder of how well-off people used to travel in China. They were replaced by faster bicycle rickshaws, but now those too are vanishing because people do not enjoy sitting in the open among the vehicle fumes.

SIGN LANGUAGE
Road signs in China all use the official written language, Mandarin Chinese. This is so that people from any region of China can read them, no matter which dialect of Chinese they speak. To help foreign visitors, some signs have a Pinyin translation in the ordinary Latin alphabet.

CHEK LAP KOK AIRPORT
Hong Kong's international airport is one of the world's busiest—a flight takes off or lands there almost every minute. It was built on a massive artificial island reclaimed from the sea and is regarded as one of the 20th century's greatest feats of engineering.

CAR CRAZY

This model is wearing a traditional costume from the Beijing Opera at one of the huge car shows in China. The shows attract thousands of visitors. More new cars are sold in China than anywhere except for Japan and the US. One reason why people in China are so excited by cars is that under the old Communist system no one was allowed to buy their own car. The first privately owned car in China took to the road in 1984.

Sports car made by the Chinese company Geely

HONG KONG TRAM

A tram system was set up in Hong Kong in 1904, when the island was a colony governed by Britain. Over a century later, Hong Kong has a fast and modern underground subway system, but the city's old-fashioned double-decker trams are still popular with the local residents.

TRANSPORTATION OF THE FUTURE?

The Shanghai Maglev train (below) accelerates to a top speed of 268 mph (431 kph), making it the fastest train service on Earth. Maglev is short for "Magnetic Levitation." Powerful magnets enable the train's wheel-less carriages to hover a few inches above a concrete runway, and the magnetic force is controlled by computers to propel the train at incredible speeds. Maglev trains were developed in England and Germany, but in 2004 China became the first country to use them for a public transportation system. The Maglev line in Shanghai is only 19 miles (30.5 km) long and was extremely expensive to build, so it is uncertain if this technology will ever replace ordinary railroads.

TRANSPORTATION CHAOS

Each spring in the days before the Chinese New Year, over 140 million people travel across China by train, bus, and air to celebrate with their families. It is the largest human migration in the world. Railroad stations are packed with noisy crowds of excited people. Many have not been home for months, or even years. After the festival, chaos takes over again as everyone makes the return journey.

Made in China

MOVING CARGO
The shipping terminal at Hong Kong is one of the busiest on the planet. It is where several Pacific Ocean trade routes meet, and it serves as a gateway for cargo to and from China and other Asian countries. Day and night, thousands of containers full of everything from T-shirts to television sets pass through the port.

IN THE 17TH CENTURY, fleets of ships carried mass-produced Chinese porcelain to sell in Europe, and throughout most of its later history China has been a major exporter of goods. But under the 20th-century Communist regime its factories were old-fashioned and inefficient. In 1978, China started to modernize its factories at last and trade with other countries grew rapidly. Now it is a leading manufacturing nation, known as the "workshop of the world." More and more people have quit farming to work in the booming manufacturing sector, and this has lifted millions of Chinese out of poverty. By 1992, China was the world's third biggest economy. It is likely to reach second place by 2015, and may overtake the US by the middle of this century.

ELECTRONICS
Most of our electronic gadgets, such as this MP3 music player, as well as most computers, TV sets, DVD recorders, cell phones, and digital cameras, are made in China.

Robotic welding arm

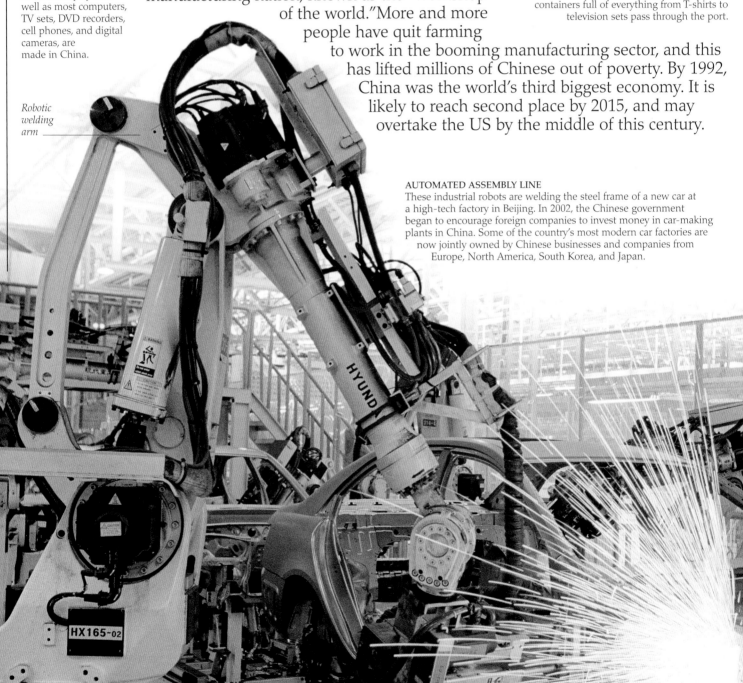

AUTOMATED ASSEMBLY LINE
These industrial robots are welding the steel frame of a new car at a high-tech factory in Beijing. In 2002, the Chinese government began to encourage foreign companies to invest money in car-making plants in China. Some of the country's most modern car factories are now jointly owned by Chinese businesses and companies from Europe, North America, South Korea, and Japan.

Old and broken bicycles for recycling

Rolled steel ready to be shipped

DEMAND FOR RAW MATERIALS
Recycling provides a valuable extra supply of raw materials for China's factories. For example, the metal in this truck-load of bicycles will be sorted and used again in a variety of new products. China also recycles waste plastic, glass, paper, and cardboard sent from as far afield as North America and Europe.

HEAVY INDUSTRY
China is the world's largest producer and importer of steel. Several million people work in its steel mills, especially in the industrial heartland in the northeast known as Dongbei. Some mills employ entire towns. The steel is used in construction and by China's giant car and truck manufacturing and shipbuilding industries.

View inside a factory owned by the Beijing Automobile Industry Corporation (BAIC) and Hyundai of South Korea

Each shoe is finished by hand

HARD WORK
Chinese workplaces vary from state-of-the-art warehouses with excellent working conditions to crowded, unhealthy "sweatshops." Most sweatshop workers are young women under 30 years old. They work long shifts making goods such as cheap shoes, clothes, and toys.

FACTORY CANTEEN
Factories in China often provide employees with meals and lodging. Migrant workers whose homes are too far away to commute every day sleep in shared dormitories at the factory. The largest factories are like small cities, with up to 200,000 people living there. Some workers may be separated from their families for a year, and return home only for the Chinese New Year celebrations.

Going to market

Oɴ ᴍᴏsᴛ ᴅᴀʏs ᴏꜰ ᴛʜᴇ ʏᴇᴀʀ ɪɴ Cʜɪɴᴀ, except for festivals and public holidays, thousands of markets are in full swing—all of them different. Each market reflects the unique character of the area and its culture and local produce. Many people visit their nearest market daily to buy fresh vegetables and meat. A huge variety of household goods can also be found there, including cotton slippers, toothbrushes, bags, woks, pots, and pans. Larger towns and cities have specialty markets for just about anything, from pet animals to carpets, trinkets, and electrical appliances. Unlike in shops, prices are rarely marked and people barter with the stallholders. In rural areas, weekly fairs are the main event in village life. Villagers visit them for social reasons and not just to go shopping.

STREET BARBER
People combine a trip to the market with other errands, such as getting a haircut from the street barber. Markets are important meeting places for local communities and a chance to catch up with one another.

ROADSIDE FRUIT SELLERS
Stallholders pay a small tax to the local government, which many poor farmers, such as these in the town of Kashgar in western China, cannot afford. Instead, they squat at the roadside to sell their produce, often charging less than normal market prices. If the police spot the street vendors they may confiscate their goods.

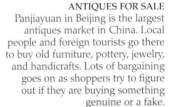

ANTIQUES FOR SALE
Panjiayuan in Beijing is the largest antiques market in China. Local people and foreign tourists go there to buy old furniture, pottery, jewelry, and handicrafts. Lots of bargaining goes on as shoppers try to figure out if they are buying something genuine or a fake.

ANIMAL MARKET
Most Chinese cities have separate flower and animal markets. Cage birds, such as these imported African lovebirds for sale in downtown Shanghai, have long been the most popular pets in China. As the incomes of city dwellers rise, more people are choosing to keep dogs and cats, and exotic pets such as aquarium fish, lizards, and turtles. Pets have a long history in China—there are paintings and statues of pet dogs dating from the Han Dynasty, and caged birds are known to have sung at concerts during the Tang Dynasty.

STEAM COOKING
This stallholder is surrounded by bamboo steamers piled high with soft, fat buns. The steamer at the front of the photograph is resting on top of a wok of boiling water. Clouds of steam rising from the wok keep the food piping hot. It is a healthy way of cooking because no oil or fat is used. Market-goers buy this kind of simple street food as a cheap snack or take it home to eat later with a meal.

BAGS OF FLAVOR
Every market has at least one trader selling dried spices and herbs. These are mixed in different combinations to create the "Five Flavors" of Chinese cooking: sweet, sour, bitter, spicy, and salty. In addition to bringing otherwise plain dishes to life, herbs and spices are valued for their health-giving properties.

Baskets of pears and plums for sale

LATE-NIGHT SHOPPING
Markets are busiest from midmorning to midafternoon, but some stay open until well into the night. During the summer many people prefer to shop in the cool of evening, particularly in the hot and humid regions of south China. The air at a night market or *yeshi* is full of the aroma of barbecued food being prepared for the hungry shoppers.

Life in the village

It CAN TAKE A DAY OR MORE to travel from a Chinese city to a remote village. When you finally arrive, it feels like stepping into another world. Here, everyone knows each other, most people are farmers, and carts pulled by donkeys or oxen may be more common than cars. China's villagers have preserved and adapted ways of cooking, farming, and building that have been handed down over generations for thousands of years. In some of the 900,000 villages in China the way of life remains unchanged, but many are affected by the rapid transformation of the country's urban areas. Millions of people are leaving the community in which they were born to work in a town or city, often far away in another province. They send home money and gifts to help older relatives and children who stayed behind. But even when life is hard, China's villagers offer a warm welcome and generous hospitality to their guests.

STAYING IN TOUCH
There are still villages in China that share a telephone like this kiosk, but rural communications are better than they used to be. Most farmers own cell phones, new apartments come with a phone line, and more schools have internet access.

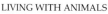

LIVING WITH ANIMALS
Chickens peck for scraps in the courtyards and mud lanes of every village in China, while many farmhouses have a room at ground level or at the back for keeping pigs. Families raise the animals to sell at market, but they keep some for feasts on special occasions. Throughout China's history pigs have been so important to the dinner table and to families' livelihoods that the Chinese character for "home" is made up from the sign for a pig under the sign for a roof.

PRECIOUS WATER
Villagers need water for drinking, bathing, doing the housework, and looking after their animals and crops. Some of China's rural areas are not linked to a water supply, so residents cannot turn on a faucet at home. Like this woman, they have to fetch water from the village well. Around 70 percent of China's rivers and lakes are polluted by industrial plants or agricultural chemicals, so lots of villages rely on deep wells that draw fresh water from far underground.

Village official speaking at a meeting

LOCAL GOVERNMENT
People in China's villages vote for their chief, but the government selects other village officials. The village leaders take important decisions, such as which crops to plant, and they sometimes organize public meetings in the school or main square to discuss local affairs.

TRADITIONAL VILLAGE
Except for its telephone wires, the village of Xijiang in Guizhou province looks much the same as it would have looked hundreds of years ago. Its wooden houses and unpaved streets are tucked onto a steep hillside close to paddy fields. On the weekend, city people visit beautiful villages like this to experience the friendly, rural way of life. Families boost their income by inviting the tourists inside for a delicious home-cooked meal.

IN SEARCH OF A NEW LIFE
Many villagers are packing their belongings and saying goodbye to their families to work in one of China's cities. More men than women make the journey, because married women may stay behind to take care of the farmwork. The migrants return only for holidays, bringing their hard-earned savings with them. People dream of saving enough to build a new house in the village or set up a business.

VILLAGE ELDERS
During the day you usually meet old people or children in villages, because everyone else is at work. The elderly are respected for their wisdom and pass village customs onto younger relatives. People today attribute this practice to Confucius, who taught that families should look up to their elders.

Farming

MORE THAN 800 MILLION PEOPLE, or around 60 percent of the population, live off the land in China. Most are peasant farmers, and the men and women alike work long hours. Today, China produces more rice, sweet potatoes, cotton, tobacco, and silk than any other country. But agriculture here is changing fast and life is more difficult for many farmers. China's cities are exploding in size and villagers are made to give their land for development, often without compensation. Other farmers have seen their fields ruined by polluted water supplies or engulfed by deserts. Millions are leaving to start a new life in cities.

HILLSIDE TERRACES
China is a vast country, but only 15 percent of its land can grow crops. Every suitable piece of land is cultivated. In mountainous regions villagers create fields by cutting terraces into steep hillsides, such as these ones growing rice in southwest China. Because land is in short supply and fields are always in use, farmers often spread out their harvest on the pavement of roads to dry.

Cotton

Sweet potato

Wheat

Tobacco

ALL KINDS OF CROPS
Farmers in China can grow a huge variety of crops because of the country's different climates. Tropical fruits thrive in the far south, but in the dry mountains of northern China people mostly grow cereal crops such as wheat, millet, and barley. Some rice farmers have switched to producing vegetables, cotton, or tobacco, which fetch a higher price at the market.

Hat and scarf protect against hot sun

MASS PRODUCTION
Commercial farming on a large scale is becoming more common in China. These workers are sorting and packing oranges in the workshop of a big food company in Zhejiang province in east China. The fruit will be sold in Chinese cities or shipped to Southeast Asia.

BEAST OF BURDEN
Many farmers use water buffalo (pictured above) or oxen to plow their fields and pull carts. These tough cattle are easier and cheaper to maintain than tractors, produce valuable manure, and can work in waterlogged fields.

Fresh mulberry leaves—the silk worms' only food

SILK FARMING
The Chinese have farmed silk since at least 3000 BCE. Silk is a soft, luxurious fiber made by carefully unraveling the cocoons spun by silk worms (actually moth caterpillars). The grubs are hatched in heated rooms and fattened up on leaves.

WORKING IN THE FIELDS
Most rice is grown in the fertile river valleys of central and southern China, especially in Yunnan province, where the hot and wet climate is ideal. Rice plants need a lot of water and are cultivated in flooded paddy fields with low mud banks to stop the water from draining away. Teams of workers tend the paddy fields by hand—a backbreaking task. China produces around one-third of all the world's rice, but it has to import extra supplies from Thailand and Vietnam to feed its growing population.

Worker plants rice seedlings one by one

SPREADING DESERT
In northwest China, years of low rainfall and overgrazing by cattle have killed off natural vegetation, and so the desert has crept farther south. As it expands, the desert buries entire villages in sand, whips up dust storms, and destroys crops. This photograph shows a mat of new grass planted by China's government to stop the march of the desert.

The natural world

Rhododendron flower

Leaves of the dawn redwood tree or Metasequoia

Chinese peony

A COUNTRY IN BLOOM

China's national flower is the Chinese peony, which is a symbol of wealth and an ingredient in traditional cures to soothe fever and prevent infections. It grows wild in Tibet and north China but is planted in gardens all around the world, together with many other Chinese plants, such as rhododendrons, azaleas, lotus flowers, and magnolia trees. Remote valleys in central China shelter an ancient type of conifer called the dawn redwood. Scientists refer to these trees as "living fossils" because their ancestors were alive 100 million years ago during the age of the dinosaurs.

WHEN THE FAR NORTH of China is gripped by fierce snowstorms, its southern provinces might bask in hot sunshine, and while one part of the country suffers from a severe drought, another area may be drenched by torrential rain. China's huge range of climates has helped create many different natural landscapes and habitats. Each habitat supports different wildlife and vegetation, and so the country is home to an astonishing variety of flora and fauna. China has around 30,000 kinds of plant, 2,500 tree varieties, 500 types of mammal, and 1,200 kinds of bird. Throughout its history China's plants and animals have given inspiration to artists, poets, and philosophers, who described the natural world as a paradise on Earth. They taught that the beauty of natural things can refresh the soul and give people spiritual enlightenment. Today, Chinese people are becoming more concerned about damage to their country's environment. There is a growing campaign to clean up polluted rivers, lakes, and air, and control the growth of sprawling cities.

SAVING THE GIANT PANDA

Giant pandas are probably China's best-loved animal and are regarded as a national treasure. These slow-moving mammals roam forests in the remote mountains of southwest China, eating almost nothing but bamboo. Decades of forest destruction and poaching mean that giant pandas are endangered in the wild, but their future might finally be secure. At conservation centers such as Wolong Panda Reserve, Chinese scientists have perfected methods of breeding giant pandas and have established a healthy captive population.

Long tail is used in male's courtship display

TOP PREDATOR

China's largest predator is the Amur tiger, named for its homeland in the Amur River region between northeast China and the far east of Russia. This is a chilly forested wilderness where deep snow blankets the ground for several months of the year. Amur, or Siberian, tigers have thicker fur than other tigers and full-grown males can weigh a massive 660 lb (300 kg). Illegal hunting has driven these magnificent cats to the brink of extinction—only 20 wild Amur tigers remain in China, with another 300–350 in Russia. Hunters sell tiger bones, whiskers, and other body parts at high prices for use in traditional Chinese medicines.

THREE GORGES DAM

In 1994, the Chinese government began work on the largest dam in the world, which spans the Yangtze River in Hubei province. The dam's water-driven turbines will generate enough electricity to power many factories and towns, but the project was heavily criticized. The vast reservoir behind the dam flooded beautiful scenery and ancient cultural sites, forced thousands of communities to leave their land, and has disrupted the local climate.

SHAGGY BEAST

Yaks are hardy, long-haired cattle native to the high plains and mountains of the Himalayas and Tibet. They are an essential resource for local people, who use yaks for transportation. Tibetans eat yak meat and blood, make butter, cheese, and yogurt from yak milk, weave rope and blankets from yak hair, and burn yak butter in their lamps. None of the animal's body is wasted. In Lhasa, Tibet's capital, Buddhist monks carve elaborate sculptures from yak butter for display during the annual Butter Lamp festival.

Shorter jaws than American alligator

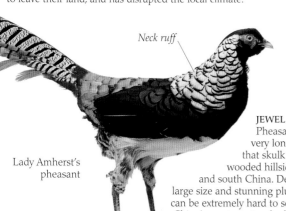

Neck ruff

Lady Amherst's pheasant

JEWEL BIRDS

Pheasants are stocky, very long-tailed birds that skulk in the densely wooded hillsides of central and south China. Despite their large size and stunning plumage, they can be extremely hard to see. Another of China's most spectacular bird families are the cranes—graceful, long-legged relatives of herons.

ENDANGERED REPTILE

The Chinese alligator (this one is a baby) is much smaller than its American relative, growing up to around 6 ft (2 m) in length. It emerges from its burrow at night to hunt fish and small aquatic animals such as mussels and snails. Fewer than 500 Chinese alligators are left in the wild, all of them in the lower reaches of the Yangtze River. They are threatened by hunting and by farming and dam-building programs, which destroy their wetland habitat.

Food and drink

CHINA HAS ONE OF THE oldest and most varied cooking traditions in the world. During the rule of emperors, banquets and tea-drinking ceremonies developed into fine arts, and to this day delicious food and drink are a national obsession in China. Cooking styles vary enormously across the country. Each region, town, and ethnic group has its own dishes and customs at mealtimes. Almost any event is an excuse for a noisy feast, and food plays an important part at every festival, family gathering, and business meeting. People eat using chopsticks made of wood, bamboo, or plastic— 45 billion pairs of disposable chopsticks were used in China each year until being banned to reduce waste.

CHANGING TASTES
Western-style fast food was unheard of in China until the late 1980s. Burger, pizza, and fried chicken outlets sprang up in big cities in the east and spread across the country.

Wooden chopsticks

Sichuan peppercorns

Red chili pepper

Food is cooked quickly in a heavy iron frying pan, or wok

Parcels of sticky rice wrapped in bamboo leaves, or zongzi

Five-spice powder

SICHUAN FLAVORS
The province of Sichuan in southwest China is famous for its fiery food based on chilis and spicy sauces. Many dishes use Sichuan peppercorns—dried lemon-scented flowerbuds that make your mouth tingle.

FESTIVE TREAT
Rice dumplings called *zongzi* are eaten during the Dragon Boat Festival to remember Qu Yuan, an ancient poet. He drowned himself in a river as a protest against corrupt government officials. Local people who knew Qu Yuan was a good man threw rice dumplings into the river so that the fish would nibble them instead.

Oolong tea

Lapsang tea

Green tea

Rose tea

Soy sauce

TYPES OF TEA
Dozens of tea (*cha*) varieties are grown in China, and some are mixed with flower petals to add fragrance and different health properties. People drink tea to relax while chatting with friends, often in teahouses.

Stretched noodles, or lai mein

EVERYDAY DIET
Rice and noodles form the basic diet in much of China. At meals everyone has a simple bowl of rice or noodles and adds meat or vegetables to it from various dishes on the table. Soy sauce, made from soybeans and roasted wheat grains, is a common ingredient in Chinese home-style cooking, used to provide a savory taste.

Bowl of sticky rice

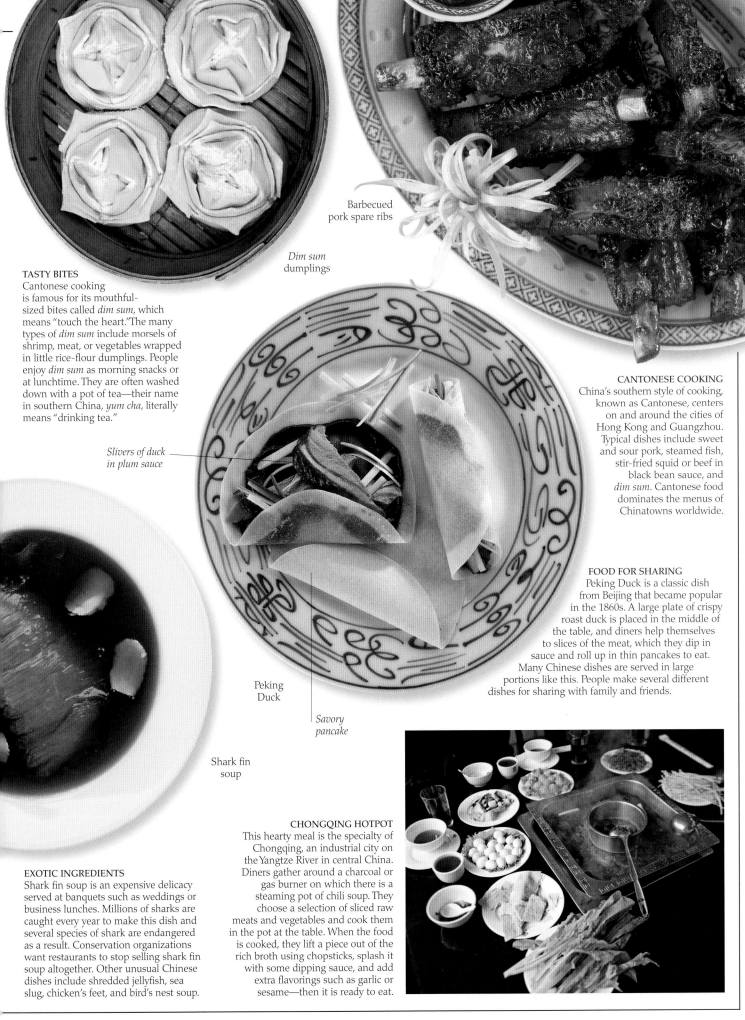

Barbecued
pork spare ribs

Dim sum
dumplings

TASTY BITES
Cantonese cooking
is famous for its mouthful-
sized bites called *dim sum*, which
means "touch the heart."The many
types of *dim sum* include morsels of
shrimp, meat, or vegetables wrapped
in little rice-flour dumplings. People
enjoy *dim sum* as morning snacks or
at lunchtime. They are often washed
down with a pot of tea—their name
in southern China, *yum cha*, literally
means "drinking tea."

*Slivers of duck
in plum sauce*

CANTONESE COOKING
China's southern style of cooking,
known as Cantonese, centers
on and around the cities of
Hong Kong and Guangzhou.
Typical dishes include sweet
and sour pork, steamed fish,
stir-fried squid or beef in
black bean sauce, and
dim sum. Cantonese food
dominates the menus of
Chinatowns worldwide.

FOOD FOR SHARING
Peking Duck is a classic dish
from Beijing that became popular
in the 1860s. A large plate of crispy
roast duck is placed in the middle of
the table, and diners help themselves
to slices of the meat, which they dip in
sauce and roll up in thin pancakes to eat.
Many Chinese dishes are served in large
portions like this. People make several different
dishes for sharing with family and friends.

Peking
Duck

*Savory
pancake*

Shark fin
soup

CHONGQING HOTPOT
This hearty meal is the specialty of
Chongqing, an industrial city on
the Yangtze River in central China.
Diners gather around a charcoal or
gas burner on which there is a
steaming pot of chili soup. They
choose a selection of sliced raw
meats and vegetables and cook
them in the pot at the table. When the food
is cooked, they lift a piece out of the
rich broth using chopsticks, splash it
with some dipping sauce, and add
extra flavorings such as garlic or
sesame—then it is ready to eat.

EXOTIC INGREDIENTS
Shark fin soup is an expensive delicacy
served at banquets such as weddings or
business lunches. Millions of sharks are
caught every year to make this dish and
several species of shark are endangered
as a result. Conservation organizations
want restaurants to stop selling shark fin
soup altogether. Other unusual Chinese
dishes include shredded jellyfish, sea
slug, chicken's feet, and bird's nest soup.

祝愿祖国富强民族昌盛

GOVERNMENT CAMPAIGN
Billboards and signs painted on walls remind people of the government's One Child policy. They often feature patriotic slogans like the one here, which says having one child will make the "motherland into a wealthy and strong nation."

Family life

PEOPLE IN CHINA PRIDE THEMSELVES on the closeness of family life. If you ask anyone why they work so hard, the answer is normally *Wei le jia*, or "For my family." Once a year, during the Qing Ming Festival in April, families visit their ancestors' graves to pay their respects, sweep clean the tombstones, and leave offerings of food and wine. Family life is affected by the government, too. In 1979, the leader Deng Xiaoping introduced the One Child policy, which says that each couple can have only one child. This was to make sure that China's population did not grow too fast. The policy has a major impact on many Chinese families—children grow up with no sisters or brothers, and parents have only one child to look after them in their old age. For young adults this can be a huge burden, because they must earn enough to support their parents and grandparents, as well as themselves.

A HELPING HAND
During the day, China's shopping malls, parks, and markets are full of grandparents looking after toddlers whose mothers and fathers are at work. In villages, where many working parents are away for over 11 months of the year, grandparents often bring up children on their own.

> *"The old house seems just a dream, but I remember vividly the warmth of home. There is no place on this Earth like home."*
>
> **DENG YUNXIANG**
> Describing his family home in old Beijing

LARGE FAMILIES
Most families in China would risk a heavy fine if they had several children, but the one-child rule does not apply to everyone. In the countryside, parents are allowed to have two children. This is because overcrowding is not a problem in rural areas, and lots of people are needed to work in the fields. Families from China's ethnic minorities can have as many children as they like. These Mongolian cattle herders need a large family to help look after their animals.

MASS WEDDING
Some couples get married in mass ceremonies, often on National Day (October 1) or a "lucky" date. The bride and groom sometimes take an organized wedding tour that includes both the ceremony and honeymoon.

INTERNET DATING
Around one-third of young Chinese people use the internet to meet their partners and future husbands or wives. In the past, arranged marriages were common. Most grandparents in China today were introduced by parents or at work by their managers.

RITUALS FOR THE DEAD
At funerals in China families sometimes burn paper models of gifts for their loved ones to use in the next world and to symbolize the wealth of the family. For example, these paper figures show members of a Hong Kong family offering cups of tea. This custom developed from a long tradition of burning paper "spirit money" at funerals to provide money for the afterlife. Mourners may also make offerings of useful items such as a toothbrush, comb, food, wine, and shoes.

FAMILY MEAL
This Shanghai family's dinner includes steamed fish, chicken, fried rice, and soup served from a hollowed-out winter melon (a savory Asian fruit). Three or four generations of the same family used to share a home and eat together, but this is less common in China now, especially in cities, where many couples have their own apartments.

Religion and spirituality

PEOPLE IN CHINA ARE OFTEN HAPPY to practice elements of different religions. They may pray at Buddhist, Daoist, and Confucian temples, as well as visit churches or mosques. The teachings of Buddha came to China from India over 2,000 years ago. In the same period, the Chinese scholar Laozi introduced the Daoist philosophy. It teaches the virtue of keeping the world in natural balance. Confucianism is based on the teachings of Confucius, who emphasized respect, kindness, and obedience. Islam has been practiced in China for over 1,000 years, and Christianity for many centuries. People of any faith may believe in the power of fortune tellers and lucky charms and in the spiritual benefits of physical exercise.

CONFUCIUS
The ideas of this great philosopher, who lived from 551 to 479 BCE, still shape what Chinese people think about the family, education, and government, and the difference between right and wrong. Confucius said that study was vital and everyone should think deeply for themselves.

LAUGHING BUDDHA
This statue of the Buddha (born c. 563 BCE) has a laughing face and fat belly, which are signs of fertility and abundance. Many Chinese people keep a statue like this in their homes, shops, or offices to bring wealth and happiness. Another common Buddhist figure in China is Kuanyin, Goddess of Mercy.

Buddha seated on a sacred lotus flower

Left arm whips to one side

TAI CHI
According to legend, *Tai Ji Quan*, or Tai Chi, was invented by a Daoist monk in the 12th century. Unlike other martial arts, it is gentle and perfomed in slow motion. Tai Chi is believed to help *Qi* (vital energy) move around the body. Many Chinese practice it as a form of healthy meditation.

Leg slides forward so that body sinks close to ground

Part of a classic Tai Chi movement

TEMPLE OFFERINGS
In the courtyard of this Buddhist temple, worshipers are saying prayers and lighting incense sticks as an offering to the Buddha. Most Chinese people—even if they are not religious—visit a temple occasionally, especially on festival days. Afterward they share a meal or pot of tea, often at an outdoor teahouse or restaurant in the temple or just outside its walls. Many people who participate in Buddhist rituals may believe aspects of other faiths too.

TIBETAN BUDDHISM
In Tibet there is a different form of Buddhism based on monasteries and led by spiritual teachers called lamas. Around one-quarter of Tibetan Buddhists live in monasteries, a tradition dating from the 16th century. The supreme Tibetan monk is known as the Dalai Lama. Tibet used to be an independent country and the Dalai Lama does not believe that Tibet should now be part of China.

Small ritual drum, called a damaru

Ritual bell, or drilbu, *represents wisdom*

Red outer robe covers a yellow inner robe

Buddhist lama

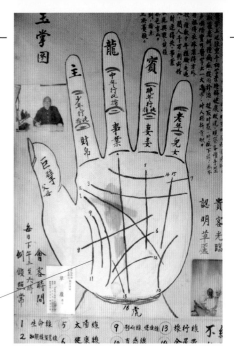

PALM READING
This sign in Hong Kong is advertising the services of a fortune teller or astrologist. Most Chinese fortune tellers begin by examining a visitor's palms and interpret the lines and creases to learn about the person's past and future. Fortune tellers also consult star charts because in China it is widely believed that your life and fortunes are related to the position of stars and planets. The usual time to visit a fortune teller is at a critical moment in your life, such as before getting married.

Each line reflects a different aspect of a person's character

HOLY COMMUNION
These girls are receiving Holy Communion from their priest at a Christmas service in a Catholic church. Around one-fifth of China's population follows Catholicism or another branch of Christianity, which is the country's fastest-growing religion. But the government places restrictions on Christians—for example, it does not recognize the authority of the pope over Catholics. In fear of persecution, many Christians meet in secret, hiding their prayer groups in private houses.

Floral garlands are worn by followers of several religions in China

Arms crossed during meditation

MUSLIMS IN CHINA
Islam is the second largest organized faith in China, after Buddhism. Most Chinese Muslims live in the northwest of the country and belong to either the Uyghur or Hui ethnic groups. The Hui people are said to be the descendants of Arabs who married Chinese people when they traded with China hundreds of years ago. Worship in China has long been isolated from religious practice overseas, so Chinese Islam has developed several unusual features of its own. Women are allowed to lead prayers in mosques, which is rare in the rest of the world.

FALUN GONG
In 1992, a Chinese man named Li Hongzhi started a new religious cult called Falun Gong. He created five sets of daily meditation exercises and introduced a set of laws and ideas similar to Buddhism. Falun Gong became massively popular, but it has been banned in China since 1999.

Festivals

THE CHINESE YEAR IS FULL of colorful festivals based on the retelling of old myths and traditional rites. Festivals are celebrated with special foods, burning incense, extravagant costumes, the loud bangs of firecrackers, street parades, and meals with the whole family. Most festivals mark important parts of the Chinese lunar calendar, which follows the cycles of the Moon and is linked to the farming year. The Chinese New Year, or Spring Festival, is the biggest party of all. It lasts around 15 days, and for three or four days the entire country closes down. Religious festivals were banned by the Communist Party, but are making a comeback. People in cities have begun to celebrate foreign festivals too, such as Halloween.

DRAGON BOAT FESTIVAL
At this summer festival teams of rowers compete in long boats decorated as dragons. The races are noisy, fast, and furious. Originally a solemn festival to remember the death of Qu Yuan, an ancient poet, this is now a fun event enjoyed by all the family.

MOON CAKES
These sweet treats are eaten during the Mid-Autumn Festival, which falls on a full Moon. They symbolize harmony, togetherness, and the Moon itself.

NEW YEAR'S EVE
The last day of the Chinese year is called *Chuxi*. Families gather to celebrate another year, visit temples to light candles, and burn incense sticks at the graves of their ancestors. The revelers eat boiled dumplings, or *jiaozi*, and in the evening every family enjoys a lavish reunion dinner. Young people are given *hongbao*—small red envelopes stuffed with money—as a symbol of wealth and good luck.

Pig 2007   Rat 2008   Ox 2009   Tiger 2010   Rabbit 2011   Dragon 2012

KHAMPA DANCERS
A group of Khampa people dance at one of the many festivals in Tibet each summer. Several times a year Tibetan people make pilgrimages (religious journeys) to places of Buddhist worship, including monasteries, temples, and sacred mountains. Pilgrims often walk for days on end to join the prayers and celebrations.

CHEUNG CHAU FESTIVAL
This bizarre spectacle takes place each May on the tiny island of Cheung Chau, near Hong Kong. For three days the islanders eat a vegetarian diet, enjoy opera and music outdoors, and dress their children up as sacred spirits. At the carnival, climbers scramble up three pillars covered with buns, which they tear off and put in a bag or throw down to the crowd.

Young men gather the buns

Tower of sweet steamed buns

CHINESE NEW YEAR FIREWORKS
All across China towns and cities stage spectacular New Year firework displays, such as this show at Victoria Bay in Hong Kong. People also set off strings of firecrackers in the street. The sound is supposed to scare away evil spirits, including *Nian*, a legendary man-eating beast. Another theory is that this custom began as a way of waking the dragon, who would create rain in the coming year and guarantee a good harvest.

CHINESE ASTROLOGY
The Chinese lunar calendar governs not only festivals, but also the practice of astrology, which attempts to foretell human destinies. Each year in China is associated with one of 12 animal signs, pictured below. These repeat in a continuous cycle. According to Chinese astrology, the sign of your birth year can reveal a lot about your character. If you were born in the "Year of the Monkey," for example, you are said to be mischievous and smart. Some parents try to plan their families so that their children are born in the year of the animals whose qualities they most admire.

Snake 2013   **Horse 2014**   **Sheep 2015**   **Monkey 2016**   **Rooster 2017**   **Dog 2018**

Education

Fine robes show high status

Scholar's scroll

Tʜᴇʀᴇ ɪs ᴀ ʟᴏɴɢ ʜɪsᴛᴏʀʏ of formal education in China. In 165 ʙᴄᴇ, the Han dynasty invented the world's first examination and introduced a civil service in which scholars governed the country. Since then education has become a major key to success. China has such a big population today that competition in school is fierce and pupils need to compete with each other to achieve. In cities, the One Child policy increases the pressure on children even more, because parents want their only child to do as well as possible. China's children start school at six or seven years old and must study until at least 14. Those who stay on spend their high school working toward the *Gaokao* (college entrance exam), a two-day event in June. For many young people, college is their first time away from home.

Laozi is often represented riding a buffalo

ANCIENT INSPIRATION
Philosophy has been an important part of education in China for 2,500 years. People still read philosophical texts for guidance in everyday life. This small bronze sculpture is of Laozi, a great thinker who lived about 2,500 years ago and whose teachings inspired the Chinese religion of Daoism. Laozi's *Tao Te Ching* contains the wisdom of living peacefully in harmony with nature.

"To learn without thinking is fruitless; to think without learning is dangerous."

CONFUCIAN SAYING
Taken from the *Analects of Confucius,*
c. 479–221 ʙᴄᴇ

COMPUTER CLASS
The best schools in China's cities offer computer lessons for children as young as six years old. Chinese computer keyboards use Pinyin—a system of writing Chinese words in the Latin (ordinary) alphabet. The computer automatically converts the Pinyin spelling to the correct Chinese characters on screen. Aside from computing, parents and pupils give top priority to science, technology, and maths. These subjects are regarded as the most useful for getting a job.

VILLAGE CLASSROOM
Eight out of 10 primary- and middle-school pupils in China attend schools in the countryside. These schools are often poor, with old buildings and basic furniture. Migrant workers who take their families to the cities with them face a worse problem. They frequently find it difficult to educate their children because the city schools are either full or too expensive.

CRAZY ENGLISH
Celebrity businessman Li Yang takes the stage in a packed meeting hall to promote *Crazy English*—his method of learning English. In his interactive public lectures Li asks his audience to shout out English phrases and chant along with him. He tells them that learning English is a big step toward improving their chances in life and developing China's economy.

Portrait of Mao Zedong

Copy of the Little Red Book

STUDYING MAO ZEDONG'S TEACHINGS
Ordinary education was abandoned in China during Mao Zedong's Cultural Revolution, which lasted 10 years. Universities were shut down by the authorities and manual labor was claimed to be more important. People such as intellectuals, professionals, and these students were forced to move to farms to learn about life on the land. Everyone in China also had to study the revolutionary teachings of Chairman Mao in his *Little Red Book*. Today, many adults who missed their chance for a good education during the Cultural Revolution pay for evening classes to learn new skills or study a foreign language.

College students perform a drill in military uniform

COLLEGE LIFE
The first two weeks at college in China are spent in military uniform learning marching and basic battlecraft. This training ends with a parade in front of army generals. Most college degrees take four years. In addition to their chosen degree subject, Chinese students must go to classes on ethics (moral behavior), the teachings of Chinese leaders, law, computers, English, and physical education.

Media

CHINA'S MEDIA REACHES OUT over huge distances to huge numbers of people hungry for information. Millions of people are avid readers of books, newspapers, magazines, and internet sites. Over 150 million people in the countryside do not know how to read. Satellite TV reaches some but not all of these rural areas. The government restricts all media, checking for any direct criticisms made against it. Despite this censorship, China's internet is home to vibrant online communities that create their own online identities, keep blogs, chat, play, and discuss the news. Many foreign internet sites are translated into Chinese, so users in China may know a lot more about the outside world than people outside may know about China.

HARRY POTTER HIT
While China has a longstanding film industry of its own, Western films, such as the Harry Potter series, are also very popular. Movie tickets are expensive, so many people download films on the internet, or watch pirate (illegally copied) DVDs.

Lights enable newspapers to be read day and night

Singdao Daily

Yangcheng Evening News

Next, a weekly magazine

PARTY NEWS
Many of China's state-owned newspapers are mounted in large, sealed frames for people to read on their way to work. Mao Zedong, who had once been a journalist, insisted that the press should act as the Communist Party's mouthpiece and publicize Party policies. Today, much of China's media earns money from advertising, reports business news, and promotes economic reform.

READ ALL ABOUT IT
There are around 2,000 newspapers in China, of which a quarter are printed by the government. The rest have private owners although their content is still heavily supervised. *Yangcheng Evening News* is the 20th best-selling newspaper in the world with a circulation of 1.7 million. *Singdao Daily*, a popular Hong Kong paper, is distributed to more than 100 cities around the world. Many of China's current affairs magazines, such as *Next*, focus on popular entertainment and the lives of the rich and famous.

BOOKS, BOOKS, BOOKS
The Chinese invented moveable type in the 11th century, which led to books becoming more widely available and more people learning to read. Today, China boasts over 400 publishing houses. Outside the big cities, mobile bookshops make regular visits to factories, mines, and villages. Official government figures show China to have a literacy rate of around 95 percent, although the figures are probably much lower in rural areas.

CHINA ONLINE
Only 8 percent of China's households own a computer, so internet cafés, which are spreading rapidly across the country, are very popular. Many stay open all night and young people often go there to relax away from home. Here, they can play games online, visit chatrooms, and download movies or music. The government controls access to foreign news through the "Great Firewall" that guards the internet gateways connecting China to the world wide web.

Viewing monitor

REALITY TV
In 1997, a small satellite TV station from Hunan province started broadcasting an American-style gameshow called *Citadel of Happiness.* It soon became one of China's most popular programs, regularly attracting around 160 million viewers. Hunan TV's own version of the smash hit *American Idol,* called *Supergirl,* attracted over 400 million viewers. Even China Central TV (CCTV), the main national network, broadcasts popular entertainment alongside government-approved news.

RURAL VIEWERS
Satellite broadcasting enables Chinese TV stations to reach large parts of China. In some villages, people can even tune into TV stations from India and other nearby countries. Eventually, the government plans to install enough satellite dishes for everyone in China to be able to watch television.

Science and innovation

MANY EVERYDAY OBJECTS AND USEFUL technologies were developed in China long before they were introduced to other countries. Early Chinese inventions include paper, printing, silk, porcelain, cast iron, kites, umbrellas, wheelbarrows, compasses, the abacus, and gunpowder. We often take these things for granted today, but they have helped to transform our world and change the course of history. During the 20th century, China earned a reputation as a workshop for Western companies where cheap goods could be mass-produced. Modern China wants to remain a major manufacturing nation, but it is also determined to honor its old position as a center of invention and discovery. Some Chinese companies are becoming global brands, while China's spaceflight program is a spectacular display of its ambition to work at the forefront of scientific progress.

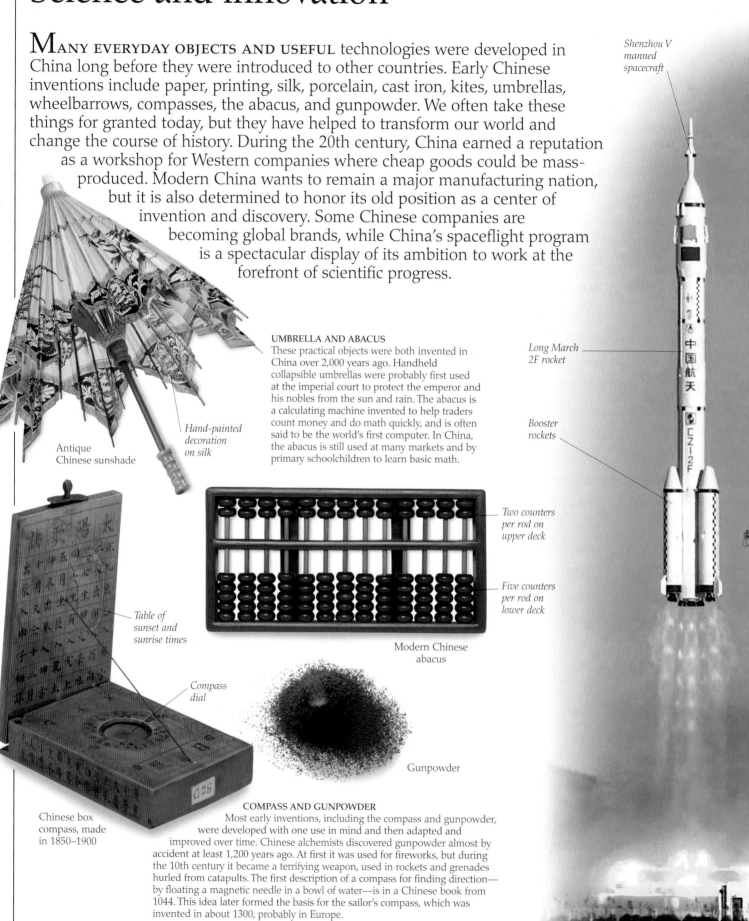

Shenzhou V manned spacecraft

Long March 2F rocket

Booster rockets

UMBRELLA AND ABACUS
These practical objects were both invented in China over 2,000 years ago. Handheld collapsible umbrellas were probably first used at the imperial court to protect the emperor and his nobles from the sun and rain. The abacus is a calculating machine invented to help traders count money and do math quickly, and is often said to be the world's first computer. In China, the abacus is still used at many markets and by primary schoolchildren to learn basic math.

Antique Chinese sunshade

Hand-painted decoration on silk

Two counters per rod on upper deck

Five counters per rod on lower deck

Table of sunset and sunrise times

Compass dial

Modern Chinese abacus

Gunpowder

Chinese box compass, made in 1850–1900

COMPASS AND GUNPOWDER
Most early inventions, including the compass and gunpowder, were developed with one use in mind and then adapted and improved over time. Chinese alchemists discovered gunpowder almost by accident at least 1,200 years ago. At first it was used for fireworks, but during the 10th century it became a terrifying weapon, used in rockets and grenades hurled from catapults. The first description of a compass for finding direction—by floating a magnetic needle in a bowl of water—is in a Chinese book from 1044. This idea later formed the basis for the sailor's compass, which was invented in about 1300, probably in Europe.

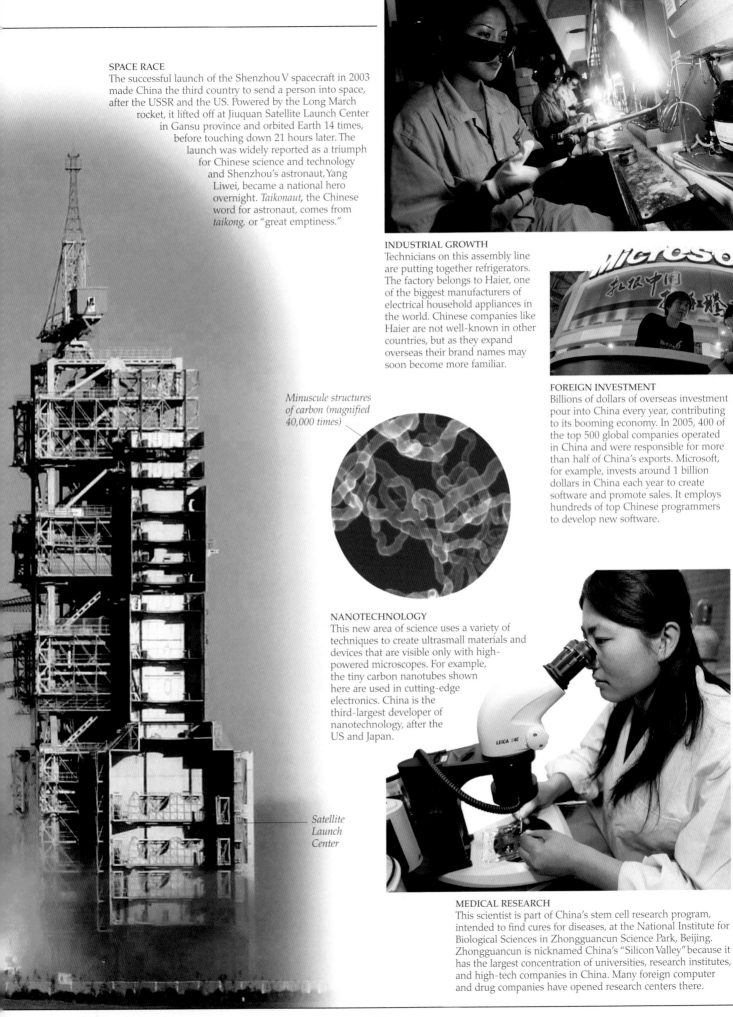

SPACE RACE

The successful launch of the Shenzhou V spacecraft in 2003 made China the third country to send a person into space, after the USSR and the US. Powered by the Long March rocket, it lifted off at Jiuquan Satellite Launch Center in Gansu province and orbited Earth 14 times, before touching down 21 hours later. The launch was widely reported as a triumph for Chinese science and technology and Shenzhou's astronaut, Yang Liwei, became a national hero overnight. *Taikonaut*, the Chinese word for astronaut, comes from *taikong*, or "great emptiness."

INDUSTRIAL GROWTH

Technicians on this assembly line are putting together refrigerators. The factory belongs to Haier, one of the biggest manufacturers of electrical household appliances in the world. Chinese companies like Haier are not well-known in other countries, but as they expand overseas their brand names may soon become more familiar.

FOREIGN INVESTMENT

Billions of dollars of overseas investment pour into China every year, contributing to its booming economy. In 2005, 400 of the top 500 global companies operated in China and were responsible for more than half of China's exports. Microsoft, for example, invests around 1 billion dollars in China each year to create software and promote sales. It employs hundreds of top Chinese programmers to develop new software.

Minuscule structures of carbon (magnified 40,000 times)

NANOTECHNOLOGY

This new area of science uses a variety of techniques to create ultrasmall materials and devices that are visible only with high-powered microscopes. For example, the tiny carbon nanotubes shown here are used in cutting-edge electronics. China is the third-largest developer of nanotechnology, after the US and Japan.

Satellite Launch Center

MEDICAL RESEARCH

This scientist is part of China's stem cell research program, intended to find cures for diseases, at the National Institute for Biological Sciences in Zhongguancun Science Park, Beijing. Zhongguancun is nicknamed China's "Silicon Valley" because it has the largest concentration of universities, research institutes, and high-tech companies in China. Many foreign computer and drug companies have opened research centers there.

Medicine and healing

TAKING CARE TO BE HEALTHY is a vital part of daily life in China. Many people use their free time to exercise regularly, and everywhere there are shops or stalls offering relaxing massages. This is believed to heal internal organs by putting pressure on certain points in the body. Chinese medicine considers the health of the entire person when diagnosing a patient, not only the part that is ailing, and poor health is attributed to emotional as well as physical problems. Treatments include herbs, acupuncture, massage, diet, and forms of exercise that promote spiritual well-being.

Yin is dark to represent the night

PRESSURE POINTS

The theory of acupuncture is that our body has around 650 pressure points, some of which are shown in this chart of the head. Every pressure point is linked to an internal organ. If needles are pushed carefully into these places, the body's *Qi* (vital energy) can flow freely to treat the illness.

YIN AND YANG

The concepts of *Yin* and *Yang* refer to two things that could not be more different from each other, and that need to be balanced to create harmony. For example, *Yin* refers to night and *Yang* to day; *Yin* concerns cold and wet things, and *Yang* concerns anything that is hot and dry. According to Chinese philosophy, the body needs a balance of these extremes to stay healthy.

Yang is white to indicate daytime

Yin Yang symbol

ANCIENT TREATMENT

Acupuncture is a method of placing sharp needles into designated points in the body to try to relieve pain and cure disease. It has been used in China for over 2,000 years, and it is still a popular therapy in hospitals and clinics. Some scientists think that acupuncture works by making the body release natural painkillers, called endorphins.

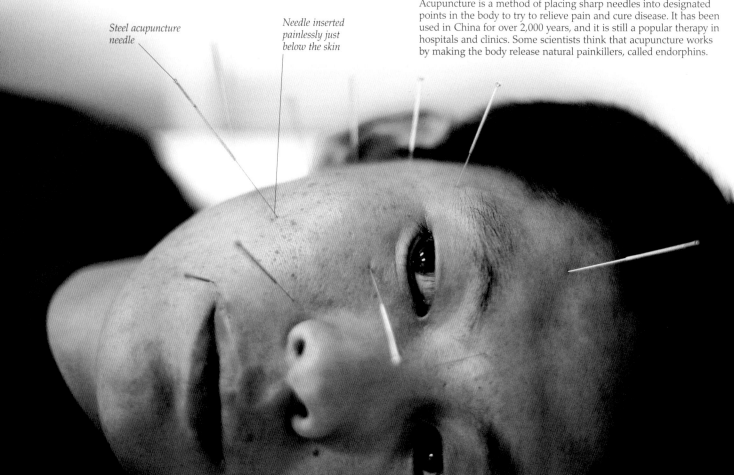

Steel acupuncture needle

Needle inserted painlessly just below the skin

RURAL CLINIC
In the countryside, small clinics provide the only medicine many Chinese have access to. The government offers only a low level of social services, so if people get sick they may have to borrow money from family or friends to pay their medical bills.

RELAX AND REFRESH
Most of China's shopping districts have booths like this, where tired shoppers or passers-by can stop for a healthy massage. Bright neon signs explain the health benefits. A popular type of massage is foot massage, or reflexology. Chinese people like to go for a foot massage with their friends after work. They soak their feet in a bowl of hot water, before lying down on a long couch to be given their massage. The practitioner applies pressure to different parts of a person's feet to improve the body's internal workings.

Ginger root, or gan jiang

Cutting board with two-handled knife

HERBAL REMEDIES
Traditional Chinese medicine is widely used to treat everything from common colds and the flu to headaches and back pain. A sick person is said to have an imbalance in the body, and the correct energy flow is restored with doses of herbs. Some of the typical ingredients in herbal remedies include roots, leaves, bark, seeds, berries, and fungi. These are usually dried, chopped, and ground into a powder using tools like those shown here.

Mortar

Pestle for grinding herbs

OLD AND NEW
This worker at a high-tech drugs company in southeast China is checking an antimalarial medicine. It contains a herb called sweet wormwood, which has been an ingredient in traditional Chinese medicines for centuries. The new drug is exported all over the world to help treat malaria, a disease spread by mosquitoes that kills 1–3 million people worldwide every year.

Mask stops germs spreading

FIGHTING DISEASE
Like any country with a huge population and crowded living conditions, China is at risk from mass outbreaks of disease (epidemics). This photograph was taken during an outbreak of the highly infectious SARS virus in China in 2003. The Chinese government spends millions of dollars a year to prevent such epidemics.

World of art

ARTISTS IN CHINA TODAY are forming their own communities, living together in disused factories in the cities or creating entire villages in the countryside. China's rich tradition of art and crafts began in imperial times, with fine ceramics, beautiful landscape paintings on paper and silk, and delicately carved sculptures in ivory, jade, terracotta (fired earth), and bronze. Writing became an art form too, known as calligraphy. During the Cultural Revolution (1966–1976), art in China was expected to fit in with the ideas of the ruling Communist Party. Many artists made propaganda—political art to help spread the government's message. Artists whose work was not considered suitable were persecuted. Since the 1980s, artists have had more freedom. Their work often reflects how life in modern China is changing.

INSPIRATION FROM NATURE
A great 16th-century artist called Wen Zhengming created this imaginary Chinese landscape using watercolor paint and ink on paper. The painting, known as *The Peach Blossom Spring*, was based on an ancient poem about a trip to paradise.

Open hand copies pose of official Mao Zedong statues

Fiberglass sculpture painted gray to look like stone

LEADER OF THE PEOPLE
In this painting, which is titled *Glorious Leader*, a group of dockyard workers gathers around Mao Zedong. The scene is painted in such a realistic style that it could almost be a photograph. It was made during China's Cultural Revolution, to encourage Chinese people to admire their leader and feel proud of their country's industrial strength.

> *"The palest ink is better than the best memory."*
>
> **CHINESE PROVERB**

HAND OF HISTORY
This dramatic sculpture by the artist Sui Jianguo represents the right arm of the leader Mao Zedong. Jianguo deliberately copied the style of the statues of Mao that the Communist Party put up all over China. He has made his sculpture enormous to suggest that Mao was a powerful figure who towered over China like a god. But the sculpture has a jagged edge and the rest of the body is missing, as if it has been torn down. The artist may be telling us that even though China's leadership has moved away from many of Mao's ideas since he died, Mao's power still hangs over Chinese people.

SHANGHAI ART SHOW
Visitors enjoy one of the hundreds of works of art on display at China's largest art show. The biannual exhibition includes sculptures, paintings, photography, video works, and live performances. Chinese artists are now much better known in the rest of the world, and international art collectors compete to buy their best pieces.

Flowing brush strokes

ANCIENT ART
Ink and wash is a highly skilled art invented in China during the 7th century, and many Chinese artists still use it to this day. Making an exquisite ink and wash sketch like this one by Xu Beihong takes a lot of concentration and years of practice. The elegant brush strokes and thin washes of ink have to be added quickly and cannot be changed afterward.

Artist made a simple home in the nest

Flowers are thrown to the watching crowd

BIRD'S NEST
This bizarre structure was erected in Beijing by art curator Zhu Qi. An artist lived in the nest for 30 days and 30 nights. Passers-by were amazed that someone could live in the open like this and it made them think about their busy lives in the city.

Steel tripod supports the nest

Mao suit, a symbol of the old Communist system in China

Music, theater, and dance

CHINA'S CULTURE IS PROBABLY more varied than ever before. People all over China still enjoy or take part in many kinds of traditional entertainment, from folk songs to Chinese opera, puppet shows, poems set to music, dragon dances, and beautiful tea-house music written to relax the mind. Meanwhile, in China's cities people have the chance to see modern ballet, concerts by the latest rock and pop stars, and plays about life in the 21st century. Often performers mix old and new styles in their work. Music and dancing are an important part of special occasions such as festivals, weddings, and funerals. They can be part of political life, too. During periods of unrest, some musicians have composed songs to support protestors demanding political changes.

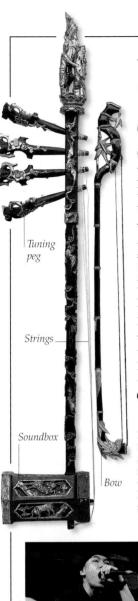

Tuning peg

Strings

Soundbox

Bow

POP PROTEST
Sometimes called the "father of Chinese rock," Cui Jian became famous in the 1980s. He was one of the first singers in China to introduce a Western rock and pop style into his songs. Some of his best-known songs were political and criticized China's leaders.

KEEPING TRADITIONS ALIVE
Some folk bands in China still play old types of instrument, such as this finely decorated 19th-century *sihu*, or spike fiddle. *Si* means four (the fiddle has four strings) and *Hu* is the family of traditional Chinese instruments to which it belongs. A *sihu* is played while held upright in the lap and is used to accompany theater and storytelling, mainly in Mongolia and northeast China.

DRAGON DANCE
In China's most spectacular and energetic dance, teams dance down the street with snakelike dragons. Beating drums and gongs set a rhythm for the dancers, who move poles to bring the colorful dragons to life. Dragon dances are a highlight of Chinese New Year and several other festivals. The dragons are magical symbols of good luck, prosperity, and fertility, and can give protection against evil spirits.

GOING UNDERGROUND
Wang Bo, a hip-hop artist from Beijing, raps with a friend at a nightclub. Singers like Wang Bo are part of China's underground urban music scene. American rap was born in poverty-stricken ghettoes, but Chinese lyrics are often about success in life.

Dragon's paper body is stretched on a lightweight bamboo frame

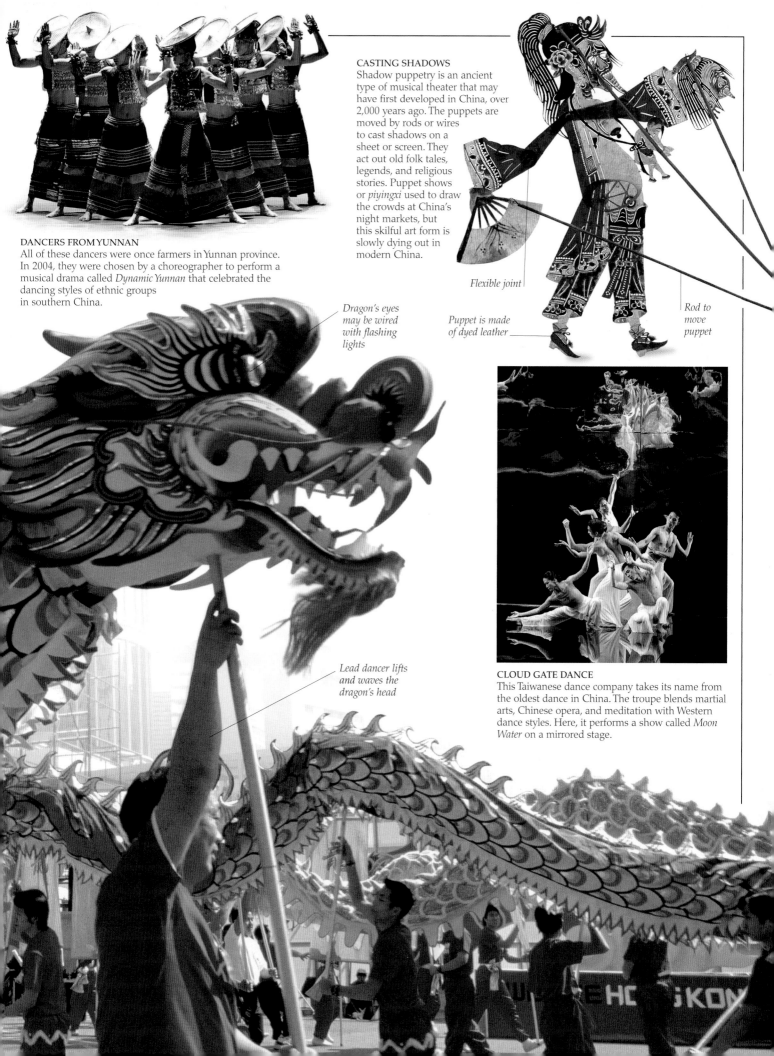

DANCERS FROM YUNNAN
All of these dancers were once farmers in Yunnan province. In 2004, they were chosen by a choreographer to perform a musical drama called *Dynamic Yunnan* that celebrated the dancing styles of ethnic groups in southern China.

CASTING SHADOWS
Shadow puppetry is an ancient type of musical theater that may have first developed in China, over 2,000 years ago. The puppets are moved by rods or wires to cast shadows on a sheet or screen. They act out old folk tales, legends, and religious stories. Puppet shows or *piyingxi* used to draw the crowds at China's night markets, but this skilful art form is slowly dying out in modern China.

Flexible joint

Puppet is made of dyed leather

Rod to move puppet

Dragon's eyes may be wired with flashing lights

Lead dancer lifts and waves the dragon's head

CLOUD GATE DANCE
This Taiwanese dance company takes its name from the oldest dance in China. The troupe blends martial arts, Chinese opera, and meditation with Western dance styles. Here, it performs a show called *Moon Water* on a mirrored stage.

Cinema

CENTURIES BEFORE THE INVENTION of movies, Chinese people had a tradition of gathering in front of a screen to be entertained by shadow puppet shows. In 1896, the first film was screened in China, starting a new era of tea-house variety shows produced in Shanghai by foreign companies. By the 1930s, China had its own film industry, which was taken over by the Communist Party when it came to power. In the late 1970s, artists who wanted to use their own imagination had to make their films secretly, away from the government censors. Today, many big-budget Chinese movies attract large audiences around the world.

SPRING IN A SMALL TOWN
The classic *Spring in a Small Town* (1948) tells the story of a woman torn between her duty to her husband and the desires of her heart. Unlike traditional Hollywood endings, Chinese love stories usually end in separation and pain, illustrating the conflict between true love and family pressures in Confucian culture.

Golden Horse statuette

CROUCHING TIGER, HIDDEN DRAGON
Ang Lee's *Crouching Tiger, Hidden Dragon* (2000) is the most successful Chinese-language film ever made, winning four Oscars. Its success inspired an international appetite for wirework-enhanced martial arts films, such as Zhang Yimou's *Hero* (2002). Some Chinese criticized these films—they felt that they were beautiful to look at but presented a stereotyped view of China.

GOLDEN HORSE FILM FESTIVAL
Taiwan's annual Golden Horse Film Festival is the Chinese-language film equivalent of the Oscars. Winners are selected after a month-long festival showcasing many of the nominated films. Hong Kong actor Andy Lau is shown here winning Best Actor for *Infernal Affairs III* (2004).

KUNG FU INDUSTRY
These all-action films, based on popular novels about legendary ancient fighters, became popular from the 1920s onward. After the Communist revolution, the Shanghai film industry moved to Hong Kong, making it the center of kung fu film production. The kung fu genre mixes Hollywood storylines with martial arts and a distinctive Chinese design, and it now has a global audience.

Posters for Western and Chinese films

BOX OFFICE
In China, a movie ticket is more expensive than going out for a meal or buying a DVD, so it is mostly well-off young people who go to the movies. China's movie theaters show mainly government-approved Chinese films alongside a fixed quota of foreign films. Starring Tom Hanks, *The Da Vinci Code* (2006) was screened for just a few weeks but it had a lot of publicity and attracted big audiences.

58

ANG LEE

Ang Lee (1954–) is a Taiwanese film director who won international acclaim with *The Wedding Banquet* (1993) and *Eat Drink Man Woman* (1994), a humorous film that looked at the awkward relationship of a Chinese restaurant chef with his daughters. When he turned 40, Lee began making movies in Hollywood. His film *Brokeback Mountain* (2005), about two American cowboys who fall in love, made him the first Asian to win an Oscar for best director.

BRUCE LEE

Bruce Lee (1940–1973) was an influential American-born martial artist. He developed his own fighting system and philosophy, known as *Jeet Kune Do*. His films, especially the Hollywood-produced *Enter the Dragon* (1973), helped to spark a major surge of interest in the West for Chinese martial arts and turned Lee into an international icon.

Sporting life

PHYSICAL FITNESS AND SPORTS ABILITY are of national importance in China, and people value sports highly for being both healthy and fun. China has a long history of martial arts, which are not only a type of combat but also a system of relaxation and exercise. China is famous too for its many world championship victories in gymnastics, badminton, table tennis, track and field, and diving. Today, sports new to the country such as golf, skiing, and Formula One racing are gaining in popularity, while older sporting events such as horse racing, dragon boat racing, and Mongolian wrestling continue to attract big crowds.

PING PONG
Table tennis does not require expensive equipment and can be played on public tables both inside and outdoors, so it is one of China's favorite sports. There are around 200 million amateur table tennis players in China, and many of the world's top pros are Chinese.

SPORTS FOR ALL
In a Chinese city no one lives far from the nearest sports facility. Neighbors exercise together using the free gym equipment arranged on many street corners, while the city council and schools provide all-weather basketball courts. Playing basketball and watching National Basketball Association (NBA) games are hugely popular pastimes in China.

Bridle is decorated with tassels and ribbons

RECENT ARRIVAL
Soccer had few fans in China until the 1980s and no professional league until 1994. Today, China is soccer-crazy. Women's soccer has more support in China than in most other countries. Players in the national women's squad can become household names.

ACROBATIC SKILL
Gymnastics is considered an art form in China, and its best gymnasts are treated as heroes. Children at the elite Shichahai Sports School in Beijing begin gymnastics training at just four years old and enter their first competitions three years later. The students must make their bodies flexible when still very young, and train extremely hard to develop their agility.

Arm outstretched to block opponent's strike

Powerful offensive kick

Kung fu students practicing their moves

SHANGHAI RACETRACK
China's desire for international prestige has led the government to build spectacular new sports arenas. Its first Grand Prix circuit opened at Shanghai in 2004. The racetrack is in the shape of the Chinese character "shang," which represents the first syllable of the city's name.

Competitor's headdress

"With strength to lift mountains and spirit to take on the world."

XIANG YU
Qin Dynasty general, 232–202 BCE

KUNG FU
Kung fu or *gongfu* means "skill." The term refers to all Chinese martial arts, including hundreds of different fighting styles from all over China. Some kung fu techniques use weapons such as swords or poles, but others rely on defensive moves or techniques to knock an attacker off balance. The town of Shaolin in Henan province in central China is full of martial arts schools that combine combat training with lessons in how to improve concentration and mental strength.

TIBETAN HORSE RACING
At the end of summer Tibetan people travel from miles around to attend horse racing competitions. The largest festival is on the Litang plain in Sichuan province, with up to 50,000 spectators. Each village chooses one rider to represent it, who races riders from all the other villages in the area.

Scarves picked off the ground by the rider as a test of skill

The end of the day

AFTER THE SUN GOES DOWN, vast areas of China turn pitch black and fall silent, but busy cities and factories light up the sky all night. Many people meet friends after work or school to enjoy a meal or perhaps watch a movie. Others head home to take care of their families. The rest work or study long into the night to boost their wages or gain new qualifications. The last thing many people do before they go to bed is wash their feet, because feet carry the body's weight around all day. Before going to sleep, people say *wan'an* to each other, which means "peaceful night." When everyone is asleep, China becomes a land of 1.3 billion different dreams. What this country will be like in the future depends much on what all these people do when they get up in the morning.

STUDYING AT HOME
Even young children in China are under pressure to study hard and get top grades so that they will end up with a good job. Primary school pupils usually do three hours of homework every night. Many also have after-school activities such as painting, Chinese chess, or music lessons.

BATH TIME
In the evening on China's older streets and alleyways people can be seen on their doorstep bathing their children, or cleaning their feet and brushing their teeth. Many homes in the countryside lack running water. Families wash in buckets of water collected from a well or filled at a public faucet.

NIGHT WORKERS
China's cities are growing so fast that many construction sites, such as here in Shanghai, are busy round the clock in the race to finish buildings on time. Chinese labor laws say that people should not work more than eight hours a day and 40 hours a week. But almost half of the workers on construction sites do overtime—they start early in the morning and continue until late at night under the glare of floodlights.

EVENING CAMPFIRE

In remote parts of China with no electricity, the day ends when the fire blows out. These Tibetan pilgrims are huddling for warmth while on a long trek to the snow-covered Mount Kailash, on the border between Tibet, India, and Nepal. For Buddhists, this holy mountain is the center of the universe, and thousands make the pilgrimage there each year.

KARAOKE FUN

One of the most popular ways to relax in China after a hard day's work is to visit a karaoke bar with friends. Karaoke began in Japan, but it spread quickly to Hong Kong and the rest of China. Today, all over the country people sing their hearts out in karaoke bars and karaoke malls, which have hundreds of private karaoke rooms to rent. The Chinese are rarely shy singers, whether at home using their own karaoke machine or in public, like this confident karaoke king.

Oriental Pearl TV tower lights up the skyline of central Shanghai

EATING OUT

Rather than cook at home, people often prefer to eat at a night market or one of the many small, cheap restaurants known as *canting* or *canguan*. These are noisy, crowded places full of laughter and the sizzling sound of fresh food being cooked. Here people catch up on each other's news away from the pressure of work or school. They order a mixture of dishes with different tastes, textures, smells, and colors. Usually people have tea or soft drinks with their meals, but groups of friends may celebrate with glasses of warm rice wine.

THE BIG CLEAN-UP

As the restaurants, bars, cafés, and night markets in a Chinese city empty of people and the city drifts off to sleep, an army of cleaners goes into action. Thousands of street sweepers work through the night to clean up the city so its ready for the next day, often using no more than a simple handmade broom and a small push cart for garbage. By 5:30 a.m. the next morning the streets will begin filling with people again.

Mapping China

At its widest point, China stretches more than 3,000 miles (5,000 km) across the Asian continent. China's landmass is approximately the same distance north of the equator and south of the North Pole as the US. It is sometimes said to be shaped like a rooster facing east, with the islands of Hainan and Taiwan as its "feet." China has many climate zones, so it experiences all extremes of weather. In much of the south and east, the average maximum temperature can exceed 86°F (30°C) in summer, but in northern regions the temperature may plunge to as low as -13°F (-25°C) in winter.

KAZAKHSTAN
Altai Mountains
Burqin
Ulungur Hu
Bohoro Shan
Yining
Urumqi
KYRGYZSTAN
Tien Shan
Aksu He
Tomiir Feng 7443m
TAJIKISTAN
Kashi
Tarim He
Korla
Bosten Hu
Kuruktag
Tarim Basin
Takla Makan Desert
Lop Nur
Ruoqiang
PAKISTAN
K2 8611m
Karakoram Pass 5575m
Altun Shan
Qilian Shan
Kunlun Mountains
Qaidam Pendi
Mt Bukan Daban 6860m
Muz Tag 6973m
Rutog
Dogai Coring
Burhan Budai Shan
Plateau of Tibet
Tongtian He
Bayan Har Shan
HIMALAYAS
C
H
Yushu
Nagqu
Qamdo
Nam Co
Nyainqentanglha Shan
Mt Xixabangma Feng 8027m
NEPAL
Lhasa
Brahmaputra
Mount Everest 8850m
BHUTAN
INDIA
MYANMAR (BURMA)

TIME ZONES

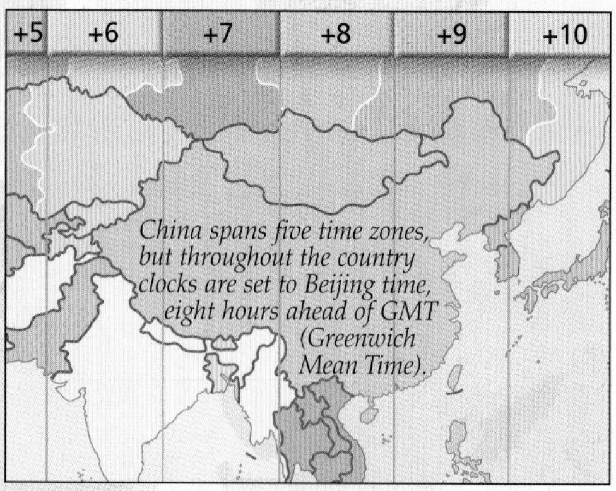

+5
+6
+7
+8
+9
+10
China spans five time zones, but throughout the country clocks are set to Beijing time, eight hours ahead of GMT (Greenwich Mean Time).

ONE COUNTRY, MANY PARTS

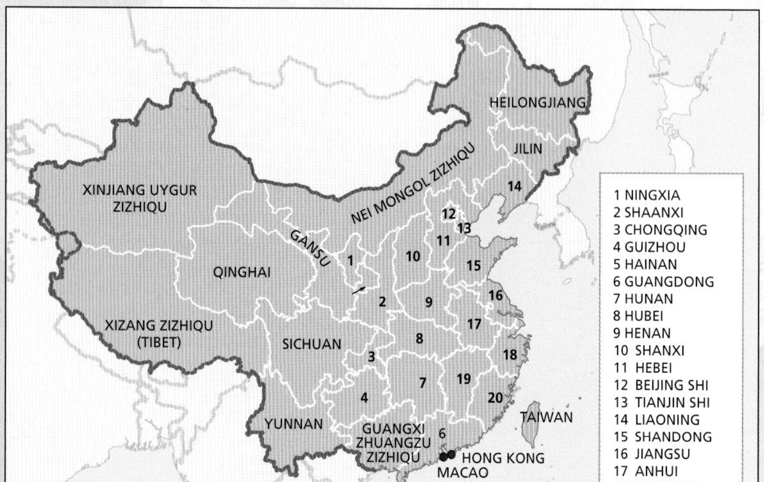

HEILONGJIANG
JILIN
XINJIANG UYGUR ZIZHIQU
NEI MONGOL ZIZHIQU
GANSU
QINGHAI
XIZANG ZIZHIQU (TIBET)
SICHUAN
YUNNAN
GUANGXI ZHUANGZU ZIZHIQU
HONG KONG
MACAO
TAIWAN
1 NINGXIA
2 SHAANXI
3 CHONGQING
4 GUIZHOU
5 HAINAN
6 GUANGDONG
7 HUNAN
8 HUBEI
9 HENAN
10 SHANXI
11 HEBEI
12 BEIJING SHI
13 TIANJIN SHI
14 LIAONING
15 SHANDONG
16 JIANGSU
17 ANHUI
18 ZHEJIANG
19 JIANGXI
20 FUJIAN

REGIONAL DIFFERENCES

China is divided into several provinces and regions (*see left*). It considers Taiwan to be one of its provinces, although this is disputed by the government of Taiwan. Tibet is administered mostly by China, but the government of Tibet in exile, headed by the Dalai Lama, denies that Tibet is part of China. Hong Kong and Macau used to be colonies of Britain and Portugal respectively, but were given back to China in 1997 and 1999. They have their own currencies (the Hong Kong dollar and the pataca) and some freedom to pass different laws from the rest of China. However, China is responsible for their defense and controls foreign affairs.

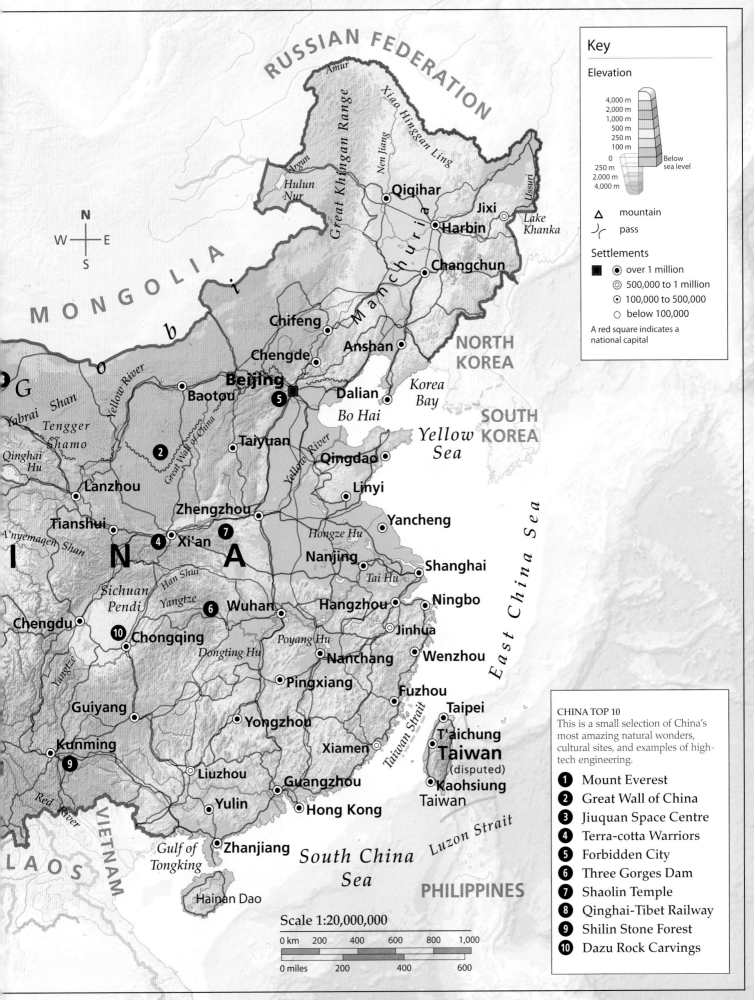

RUSSIAN FEDERATION

Amur

Argun

Xiao Hinggan Ling

Nen Jiang

Great Khingan Range

Hulun Nur

◉ Qiqihar

● Jixi

● Harbin

◉ Lake Khanka

Ussuri

Manchuria

● Changchun

MONGOLIA

Yabrai Shan

Tengger Shamo

Qinghai Hu

O G

◉ Chifeng

Chengde ◉

■ Beijing

⑤

◉ Baotou

Dalian ◉

NORTH KOREA

Korea Bay

Bo Hai

SOUTH KOREA

◉ Taiyuan

◉ Qingdao

Yellow Sea

②

Yellow River

Great Wall of China

◉ Lanzhou

◉ Linyi

● Zhengzhou

Yellow River

◉ Tianshui

④ ● Xi'an

⑦

◉ Yancheng

I N A

A'nyemaqen Shan

Han Shui

● Nanjing

◉ Shanghai

Hongze Hu

East China Sea

Tai Hu

● Chengdu

Sichuan Pendi

Yangtze

⑥ ● Wuhan

● Hangzhou

◉ Ningbo

⑩ ● Chongqing

Poyang Hu

◎ Jinhua

Dongting Hu

● Nanchang

◉ Wenzhou

● Pingxiang

● Fuzhou

● Guiyang

◉ Yongzhou

● Taipei

◎ T'aichung

Taiwan

(disputed)

● Kunming

◉ Xiamen

⑨

◎ Liuzhou

● Kaohsiung

Taiwan

● Guangzhou

Red River

● Yulin

Taiwan Strait

VIETNAM

● Hong Kong

Gulf of Tongking

◉ Zhanjiang

South China Sea

Luzon Strait

LAOS

PHILIPPINES

Hainan Dao

Key

Elevation

4,000 m
2,000 m
1,000 m
500 m
250 m
100 m
0
250 m
2,000 m
4,000 m

Below sea level

△ mountain

pass

Settlements

■ ◉ over 1 million

◎ 500,000 to 1 million

◉ 100,000 to 500,000

○ below 100,000

A red square indicates a national capital

CHINA TOP 10
This is a small selection of China's most amazing natural wonders, cultural sites, and examples of high-tech engineering.

① Mount Everest
② Great Wall of China
③ Jiuquan Space Centre
④ Terra-cotta Warriors
⑤ Forbidden City
⑥ Three Gorges Dam
⑦ Shaolin Temple
⑧ Qinghai-Tibet Railway
⑨ Shilin Stone Forest
⑩ Dazu Rock Carvings

Scale 1:20,000,000

0 km   200   400   600   800   1,000

0 miles   200   400   600

Timeline

SOME HISTORIANS TODAY SEE CHINA'S imperial past as a series of cycles. Each dynasty had its moment of power before it faded. China has been conquered by many new masters and absorbed them. It has been through periods of bloodshed and famine followed by order and prosperity. To many Chinese, modern progress is just another cycle. Whatever the future holds, China has always had the vitality that survives change.

19th-century lacquered-wood cabinet, Qing Dynasty

600,000 BCE
Said to be the earliest human remains, "Peking Man" dates from this time.

10,000–3000 BCE
During the Neolithic period, farming villages are established along the banks of the Yellow, Yangtze, and Huai rivers.

3000–221 BCE
In contrast to Europe during the Bronze Age, the Chinese do not use bronze to make farming tools, but for elaborate ornaments for use in ritual ceremonies.

c. 1650–1027 BCE
Rule of the Shang, China's earliest dynasty. Its rulers introduce the practice of ancestor worship.

1027–481 BCE
Under the Zhou Dynasty, the feudal dukes of Zhou rule over numerous feuding kingdoms.

Terra-cotta soldier, Han Dynasty

481–221 BCE
During the Warring States period, the great dukes fight each other for supremacy as the Zhou Dynasty goes into decline. Confucius, Laozi, and other scholars teach harmony and peace as an alternative way of life.

221–207 BCE
The ruler of Qin unites China and becomes its first emperor, the Qin shihuangdi. He builds the first Great Wall to protect his empire against invaders and fence in his subjects. He holds the empire together by establishing a standard system of Chinese writing, currency, and measurements, along with a central administrative system. The 8,000-strong terra-cotta army that guards the First Emperor's tomb was one of the greatest archeological discoveries of the 20th century.

207 BCE—220 CE
The Han Dynasty overthrows the Qin and strengthens imperial rule by introducing a civil service examination and establishing a bureaucratic hierarchy that runs China for the next 2,000 years. The capital, Chang'an, is one of the two largest cities in the world at this time, alongside Rome. The development of iron tools, such as plows, enables agriculture and industry to progress rapidly. Paper making is developed, too.

221–618 CE
Another period of disunity is followed by the rule of the Sui Dynasty, which reunifies north and south China. Buddhism makes its mark in China during these turbulent years.

618–960 CE
During the Tang Dynasty, the Chinese empire expands into a great world power. In this period of prosperity, merchants from all over the world flock to Chang'an, now the world's largest and wealthiest city. Poetry, music, and painting flourish. The civil service examination is improved to ensure that officials are recruited by merit rather than by birth. The period of invasion, rebellion, and disunity after 907 CE is known as the Five Dynasties period.

960–1279
China is united once more under the Song emperors. This period is characterized by great advances in science and technology, along with poetry and painting.

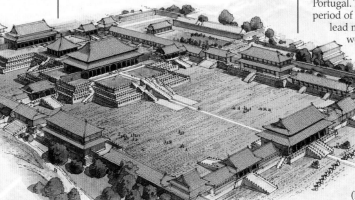

The central section of the Imperial Palace complex in Beijing, known as the Forbidden City. Dating from the 5th century, the Palace has 800 buildings with 8,000 rooms.

1279–1368
China is conquered by the Mongols under Genghis Khan. The Yuan Dynasty is founded by his grandson, Kublai Khan. International trade flourishes as China takes control of a series of overland trading routes with the Middle East, known as the "Silk Road." The Great Canal is built in eastern China, linking the Yangtze and Yellow rivers. A new capital is established at Dadu (Beijing). Many Europeans, such as Marco Polo, visit China, returning home with Chinese inventions, such as gunpowder.

1368–1644
The Chinese drive the Mongols out of China and the Ming Dynasty takes power. The Ming emperors build a new Great Wall and improve the Grand Canal. Their dynasty becomes famous for its exquisite arts and crafts. China attempts to extend its influence abroad by sending Admiral Zheng He on several great maritime expeditions to Asia and Arabia between 1405 and 1433. By the 17th century, Chinese porcelain and other luxury goods become highly sought after by the Europeans.

1644–1912
The Qing Dynasty, led by the non-Chinese Manchu, takes power. During the 19th century it goes into decline, due to financial difficulties and internal political conflicts. After a series of wars with foreign powers, starting with the First Opium War (1839–1842), China is forced to yield trading concessions and territory. It hands over Hong Kong to Britain and Macau to Portugal. These humiliations begin a long period of Chinese suspicion of the West and lead many Chinese to view their rulers as weak and corrupt.

1899–1901
The Boxers—a religious sect from north China—spread hatred of foreigners. They form an alliance with Empress Dowager Cixi and trigger the Boxer Rebellion by attacking Westerners in China and killing thousands of Chinese Christians. The uprising ends with the occupation of Peking (Beijing) by 20,000 foreign troops.

1911
The Chinese Revolution overthrows the Qing Dynasty, replacing it with the Republic of China. Its first president, Sun Yat-sen, founds the ruling Kuomintang (KMT) Nationalist Party.

1912–1919
Regional warlords struggle for power in China. The political instability leads intellectuals to form the May Fourth Movement in 1919, which seeks a new direction for Chinese politics and culture. Attracted to socialist ideas, some of the movement's leaders, including Mao Zedong, found the Chinese Communist Party (CCP).

1926
Following Sun Yat-sen's death the previous year, General Chiang Kai-shek takes over as KMT leader. The KMT fights against the warlords.

Trainees at an imperial army school during the Boxer Rebellion of 1898–1901

1927–1949
Chinese civil war starts after Chiang's attempt to crush the Communists in Shanghai.

1934–1935
KMT troops attempt to trap the Communist army in its base in southern China, forcing it to escape into the mountains. During this retreat, known as the Long March, Mao Zedong assumes leadership of the CCP.

1937–1945
Japan occupies Manchuria in northeast China, causing a war that China eventually wins.

1949
The KMT loses China's civil war and flees to the island of Taiwan, where Chiang sets up a rival government. On the mainland, Mao founds the People's Republic of China (PRC).

US president Richard Nixon with Zhou Enlai, Mao's adviser, during Nixon's historic visit to China in 1972

1950–1953
China enters the Korean War in support of the communist-ruled North Korea.

1953–1963
Chairman Mao launches the First and Second Five Year Plans, also known as The Great Leap Forward. His goal is to transform China from an agricultural to an industrial nation as quickly as possible. But these policies come at a huge cost to China's people. For example, the disruption to farming causes massive shortages of food and up to 30 million people die of hunger.

1964
China carries out its first nuclear weapons test.

1966–1976
Mao launches the Cultural Revolution in an attempt to defeat his political rivals, strengthen support for his ideas, and destroy the past. He uses a movement of young people, known as the Red Guards, to spread the revolution and round up his enemies.

1976–1997
After Mao's death in 1976, Deng Xiaoping takes power. Deng introduces economic reforms that encourage private enterprise and open up China's economy to foreign investment.

1989
Massive student demonstrations in Tian'an Men Square, Beijing, demand political reforms. This is the largest urban protest movement ever seen in China, but it is crushed by the government.

1995
China's economy reaches double-digit growth.

1997
In June, the UK returns Hong Kong to China.

2001
China enters the global economic community by accepting membership of the World Trade Organization (WTO).

2003
China launches its first manned space mission. It becomes the third country into space, after the USSR and US.

2004
China changes its constitution to recognize the private ownership of property.

2006
Hu Jintao, who takes over as premier in 2003, presents his idea of a "Harmonious Society." This is a bid to solve China's growing gap between rich and poor and between its cities and the countryside.

2008
Beijing hosts the Olympic Games.

Hu Jintao addressing a regional forum in 2006

This propaganda painting, titled *The Revolutionary Ideal is Supreme*, depicts a scene from the Long March (1934–1935), which played a crucial role in establishing Mao Zedong's leadership and Communist support.

Famous Chinese

DURING THE 20TH AND 21ST CENTURIES, Chinese people have excelled in all walks of life—as politicians, generals, directors, actors, singers, sports stars, businesspeople, novelists, scientists, inventors, artists, and architects. Many of them have become international icons. Towering above them all is Mao Zedong, one of the century's most controversial leaders and founder of the world's longest-lasting Communist regime.

SUN YAT-SEN (1866–1925)
Revolutionary leader who played a key role in toppling the Qing dynasty in 1911. Co-founder of the Kuomintang (KMT) Nationalist Party, he became its first leader and the first president of the Republic of China. Today, he is equally revered in China and Taiwan, where he is known as the "Father of the Nation."

CHIANG KAI-SHEK (1887–1975)
Leader of the KMT after Sun Yat-sen's death. By 1928, he had defeated the warlords and emerged as overall leader of China. After dealing with Communist bandits in 1934, he found himself fighting on several fronts, against rival challengers within the KMT, and then against Japanese forces after they invaded China in 1937. The war against Japan strengthened Chiang's position and his international stature grew with US support. However, after 1945, Chiang became involved in a full-scale civil war with Mao's Communist forces, which he lost. In 1949, he retreated to Taiwan, where he founded an alternative Republic of China.

Jiang Qing, member of the "Gang of Four," appearing in court in 1980

MAO ZEDONG (1893–1976)
Son of a wealthy farmer from Hunan, Mao joined the Communist Party in his late twenties. In 1934, he emerged as the top Communist leader during the Long March, when he escaped to safety with his men and managed to get rid of his rivals. Following Communist victory over the KMT during China's civil war, Mao founded the People's Republic of China on October 1, 1949. During his rule, the Communist Party assumed control of all media, which they used to promote the image of Mao and the Party. In 1958, Mao began a program of rapid industrialization that was to prove disastrous, since up to 30 million people starved from widespread famine, after all private food production was banned. In 1966, he launched the Cultural Revolution in order purge his political rivals, and again plunged the country into chaos. He spread his ideas by distributing millions of copies of his *Little Red Book* across the country and encouraged gangs of fanatical young people, known as Red Guards. After Mao's death in 1976, the reformer Deng Xiaoping won the ensuing power struggle for leader. Today, Mao's personality cult is still strong and his presence hovers over China. Many consider him to be one of the 20th century's worst dictators.

QIAN XUESEN (1911–)
Considered the father of China's space program. An American-trained nuclear physicist who studied missile technology, Qian was expelled from the US in 1955 for suspected Communist sympathies. He helped create China's first ballistic missile, and his research was used as the basis of the Long March rocket.

JIANG QING (1914–1991)
Chairman Mao's fourth wife and member of the "Gang of Four." Jiang gained notoriety for her leading role in the Cultural Revolution. At her trial she defended herself by saying: "I was Chairman Mao's dog. Whoever he asked me to bite, I bit." She was given life imprisonment in 1980 and killed herself in prison.

Jackie Chan in a scene from *Rush Hour* (1998)

I. M. PEI (1917–)
Internationally acclaimed modernist architect. Born in Guangzhou, Pei studied in the US, where he now lives. Using mainly concrete, glass, and steel, his buildings include the Bank of China Tower in Hong Kong (1982–1990) and the Louvre Pyramid in Paris (1989).

I. M. Pei's glass pyramid in the Louvre Museum Courtyard

Wang Fei wins "Best Female Artist" at the 2004 Golden Melody Award in Taiwan

LI NING (1963–)

A gymnast who won three golds, two silvers, and a bronze at the 1984 LA Olympics. During his 19-year career, Li won over 100 medals, boosting China's reputation as a great sporting nation. When he retired in 1988, he set up a successful sports brand named after himself. It now has thousands of outlets across China.

YANG LIWEI (1965–)

A national hero in 2003 after becoming the first Chinese *taikonaut,* or astronaut, to be sent into space. A colonel in the People's Liberation Army, Yang orbited the Earth 14 times in 24 hours in the Shenzhou V spacecraft, launched by the Long March rocket. Its launch was considered a triumph for Chinese technology.

WANG DAN (1969–)

Student leader of the 1989 Tian'an Men Square movement. He was arrested and sentenced to prison twice, in 1989 and 1995, for conspiring to overthrow China's Communist Party. He spent seven years in prison but was exiled to the US in 1998 following international pressure.

WANG FEI A.K.A. FAYE WONG (1969–)

A Hong Kong pop diva and world's best-selling star of Canto-Pop (sung in Cantonese). More recently, she has started writing her own more Western-influenced songs. She is also a famous actress, with roles in such films as *Chungking Express* (1994) and *Chinese Odyssey 2002* (2002).

DENG YAPING (1973–)

A sportswoman who won four Olympic Gold medals for China's female table tennis team and successfully defended her world champion title 18 times. In 1999, she was voted Chinese female athlete of the century.

ZHANG ZIYI (1979–)

A world-famous actress who began her film career in Zhang Yimou's *The Road Home.* Working with renowned directors like Ang Lee, Wong Kar-Wai, and Rob Marshall, she has played lead roles in films such as *Crouching Tiger, Hidden Dragon* (2000), *House of Flying Daggers* (2004), *2046* (2004), and *Memoirs of a Geisha* (2005), for which she was nominated for a Best Actress BAFTA. She was the youngest-ever jury member at the Cannes Film Festival.

YAO MING (1980–)

A professional basketball player who plays for the Houston Rockets in the NBA league. Standing 7ft 6 in (2.3 m) tall, he is one of the top center players in the world and has been voted an NBA All Star four times.

Li Ning won six medals at the Los Angeles Olympics, including two golds

LI KA-SHING (1928–)

Industrial tycoon who started off as a salesman in Hong Kong, before building a business that includes construction, property, banking, cement, communications, plastics, stores, hotels, airports, electric power, ports, shipping, and steel. He is the richest Chinese person in the world and has set up a foundation giving money to education, health, culture, and community projects.

GAO XINGJIAN (1940–)

A Nobel Prize-winning novelist who has lived in Paris since 1988. *Soul Mountain* (1990) is Gao's most famous work; it uses different narrative voices to tell the story of a person traveling to a mountain in China called Lingshan. When he won the Nobel Prize in 2000, some Chinese critics spoke out against his nomination since his work is not recognized in China. He is also a playwright, translator, painter, and stage director.

ZHANG YIMOU (1951–)

A leading director, Zhang spearheaded the "fifth generation" of filmmakers who took Chinese films to international audiences. Early low-budget films, like *The Road Home* (1999) and *Ju Dou* (1990), highlighted problems in China's countryside and cities. More recent historical epics, such as *Hero* (2002) and *House of Flying Daggers* (2004), are admired for their beautifully choreographed combat scenes and rich use of color. Zhang was chosen to direct the opening ceremony of the 2008 Beijing Olympics.

JUNG CHAN (1952–)

An award-winning writer now living in the UK. Her international best-seller, *Wild Swans* (1992), tells the story of three generations of women (her grandmother, mother, and herself) living through the upheavals of 20th-century China.

JACKIE CHAN (1954–)

A well-known singer, actor, stuntman, kung fu star, director, and scriptwriter, Chan now works mainly in Hollywood. He has released more than 20 albums in Asia and sings the theme tunes to many of his films. He also has his own cartoon series.

Yang Liwei being interviewed live from space

Deng Yaping going for gold

Glossary

Calligraphy characters representing a woman (left) and man (right)

ACUPUNCTURE A system of healing practiced since ancient China. Fine needles are inserted into specific pressure points around the body to stimulate the body's natural flow of energy or *Qi*, to relieve pain or treat a variety of medical conditions.

ASTROLOGY The attempt to tell the future from the planets. Chinese astrology is based on the Chinese calendar. The 60-year cycle contains 12 zodiac animals, such as the dragon, horse, monkey, rooster, dog, pig, and rat, each with five possible elements. People born in an animal's year are supposed to inherit its characteristics.

BAMBOO A tall, tropical or semitropical fast-growing grass with hollow woody stems and edible young shoots.

BUDDHA Title given to Siddhartha Gautama (c. 563–483 BCE), a nobleman and religious teacher from north India who devoted his life to seeking spiritual enlightenment.

BUDDHISM Religious teaching spread by Buddha and his followers from the 5th century BCE onward. It suggests humankind can attain enlightenment and peace by avoiding greed and hatred. It is one of China's main religions and the world's fourth largest, with 360 million followers around the globe.

CALLIGRAPHY A style of beautiful, flowing handwriting created with ink and pens and brushes of different shapes and sizes.

CANTONESE Chinese dialect spoken mostly in Guangdong province, Hong Kong, and Macau; also refers to this area's people and to its style of Chinese cooking.

CHINESE NEW YEAR *see* Spring Festival

CHOPSTICKS Pair of long, thin wooden implements used for eating.

CIVIL WAR War between people or groups from different regions of the same country. In China, it refers to the conflict in 1927–1937 and 1945–1949 between the Kuomintang (KMT) forces led by Chiang Kai-shek and the Communist forces of Mao Zedong.

COMMUNE Refers to a group of families or individuals living together and sharing their possessions and responsibilities. During Mao's "Great Leap Forward," the policy of collectivization meant that agricultural workers were forced to live together in enormous communes.

COMMUNISM Political system that aims for an equal, classless society in which private property is banned and the community owns industry and farming.

COMMUNIST PARTY In China, this is the single, ruling political group, often known simply as the "Party."

CONFUCIANISM Philosophy based on the teachings of Confucius, a major influence on the political, social, and cultural life of China. It forms the basis of Chinese education and emphasizes moral order, obedience, and the importance of the family.

CONFUCIUS Ancient Chinese philosopher who lived from 551 to 479 BCE. He has been revered as a great sage and teacher of morals and used by rulers to legitimize government.

CULTURAL REVOLUTION Movement launched by Mao Zedong that was intended to defeat his political rivals, strengthen support for his ideas, and destroy the past. It lasted from 1966 to 1976 and was enforced by a mob of fanatical young volunteers, known as the Red Guards.

Communist memorabilia: Mao Zedong badges

DAOISM Philosophy based on the teachings of Laozi, who lived at some time between the 4th and 6th centuries BCE. It promotes a simple, honest life and warns against interfering with the natural flow of events.

DIALECT Form of language spoken in a particular region. There are hundreds of dialects spoken in China, such as Cantonese (see left) and Wu (used mostly in Shanghai and nearby areas of southeast China).

DIM SUM Small Chinese snacks, normally to accompany tea—often steamed dumplings with fillings like pork, shrimp, or vegetables.

DYNASTY A sequence of hereditary rulers from the same family; in imperial China, it refers to a succession of related emperors from the same family or ethnic group, such as the Ming.

Dim sum

FENG SHUI Ancient Chinese art of designing buildings and graves to achieve harmony within the natural environment. It aims to maximize the flow of *Qi*, or "natural energy," thereby bringing good fortune.

HAN The main ethnic group within China, to which approximately 90 percent of the country's population belong.

HUTONG Old alleyway in Beijing and other northern cities, lined with courtyard houses. Originally a Mongol term, meaning "where people live."

KUNG FU Chinese martial art based on self-defense and training both body and mind; popularized by the films of actor Bruce Lee.

KUOMINTANG (KMT) A political party founded by Sun Yat-sen in 1911 and which dominated China from around 1928 to 1949 under the leadership of Chiang Kai-shek. In 1949, Communist forces drove the KMT into exile in Taiwan, where it became the ruling party. Also known as the Nationalist Party.

Kung fu practitioner demonstrates a balanced defensive move

Mandarin "Good luck" greeting on a Chinese New Year gift

MANDARIN China's official national language since 1917, spoken by around two-thirds of the population. It is used by China's television, radio, and newspapers, and is taught in schools around the country.

MAO SUIT A simple style of cotton clothing that resembles a military uniform and consists of loose pants and a jacket. It was worn by most people in Communist China during the 20th century, but is seen less often today.

MIGRANT A person who moves from one place to another, often for economic reasons and often from the countryside to the city or another country.

MILLET A cereal grass cultivated for grain and animal fodder; the grain can be boiled for cereal or ground for flour.

NATIONALIST PARTY *see* Kuomintang

NOMAD Member of a tribe or people, often with livestock, who move around to search for pasture or food.

PADDY FIELD A well-irrigated field used for growing rice, especially in China and the rest of southeast Asia.

PICTOGRAM A picture or symbol that is a drawing of the word or words it represents, as used in written Chinese.

PINYIN System of spelling used to translate Chinese characters into the Latin (ordinary) alphabet so that they can be read by speakers of European languages, such as English.

PORCELAIN Translucent ceramic made from clay, ground glass, and ash. Its fine, delicate finish made it a highly desirable export for European traders.

PROPAGANDA Organized system for spreading information, intended to promote a particular point of view for political ends.

QI (CHI) According to Eastern philosophy, the vital energy believed to circulate around the body in currents called meridians.

RENMINBI (RMB) *see* Yuan

REVOLUTION Significant change, including overthrow of a governing regime.

RICKSHAW A small, two-wheeled passenger vehicle pulled by one or two people, used in parts of Asia. Modern pedicabs are equipped with a bicycle or a motorcycle engine.

SILK WORM A white caterpillar of the Chinese silk worm moth, and the source of most commercial silk.

Curved base reflects heat evenly

Stir-frying vegetables in a wok

SPRING FESTIVAL The most important Chinese festival, which celebrates the Chinese New Year. It falls on the first day of the first lunar month (usually around a month later than in the Western calendar) and lasts for 15 days. It is a time for all the family to come together, and includes a seven-day holiday.

TAI CHI A form of exercise that uses slow, graceful, rhythmic movements based on the martial arts and developed since ancient China. It is often used as a form of spiritual meditation.

A selection of Chinese paper currency. China's currency is called *yuan*

TERRA-COTTA A reddish-brown clay that is fired but not glazed.

TRADITIONAL CHINESE MEDICINE (TCM) A healing tradition that emerged in ancient China, based on the manipulation of the body's "natural energy" or *Qi*. It uses herbs, acupuncture, massage, various forms of exercise, and diet.

WOK A large, round, metal Chinese cooking pot with a curved base.

YIN AND YANG Refers to the Chinese belief that within everything there are always two natures—*Yin* and *Yang*—which are complementary and balance each other. For example, *Yin* refers to things that are dark, cold, wet, and feminine, whereas *Yang* refers to bright, hot, dry, and masculine things.

YUAN The main monetary unit of China, divided into 10 *jiao* and 100 *fen*. Also known as *renminbi* or RMB.

YURT A circular tent with a frame of poles covered by felt or canvas, used by Mongolian and Turkic nomads from East and Central Asia. Also known as a *ger*.

Paddy fields for rice cultivation in southwest China

Index

Acknowledgments

The author would like to thank:
Frances Baawuah, Edera Liang & family, Nicholas Gerda, Coral & Dominic Sebag-Montefiore, Chen Songzhu, Melanie Williams, Duan Yanling, Dominic Zeigler.

The publisher would like to thank:
Claire Bowers, David Ekholm–Jälbum, Sunita Gahir, Joanne Little, Susan St Louis, Steve Setford, & Bulent Yusef for the clip art; David Ball, Kathy Fahey, Neville Graham, Rose Horridge, Joanne Little, & Sue Nicholson for the wall chart; Phil Hunt & Nigel Ritchie for editorial assistance; Andy Hilliard, Ben Hung, Ronaldo Julien, & David Meier for DTP support; Lynn Bresler for proof-reading & the index; Margaret Parrish for Americanization.

The publisher would like to thank the following for their kind permission to reproduce their photographs:

a-above; b-below/bottom; c-center; l-left; r-right; t-top

akg-images: 11tr, 12tl; **Alamy Images:** Pat Behnke 14cl, 38bl, 63cr; Tibor Bognar 42b; Marco Brivio 30b; Mehdi Chebil 17cr, 32br;

Cosmo Condina 68bl; Content Mime International 68cr; Dennis Cox 6-7bc; James Davis Photography 27tr; Kevin Foy 31tl, 60cl, 62b; James Frank 19br; Robert Fried 10tr; Mike Goldwater 63bc; Sally & Richard Greenhill 41b; Robert Harding Picture Library Ltd. 9c; imagebroker 9cr; Norma Joseph 21cr; Lou Linwei 19tr, 41cla, 43cr; Tina Manley 39br; Iain Masterton 43tr, 48bl, 53br; nagelestock.com 11b; David Noton Photography 8-9b; Panorama Media (Beijing) Ltd. 34cl; Phototake Inc. 51c; Jiri Rezac 19tl; rochaphoto 40tl; Marco Secchi 30cr; Keren Su / China Span 36bl; Jeremy Sutton-Hibbert 23br; vario images GmbH & Co.KG 27tl; Visual Arts Library (London) 10bl, 47tr; WorldFoto 27b, 30tl; **The Bridgeman Art Library:** Musée Guimet, Paris 46tr; Private Collection 12bl, 54cla; Private Collection / Archives Charmet 67bl; Private Collection / Photo © Christie's Images 54tl; **Corbis:** 67tr; K. Andrew / epa 37cl; Dave Bartruff 12c; Annie Griffiths Belt 22cr; Bettmann 12cl, 13c, 68clb; Bohemian Nomad Picturemakers 62tl; Adrian Bradshaw / epa 49b; Tom Brakefield 37tr; Brooklyn Production 40cla; David Butow / Corbis Saba 16-17bc; Kin Cheung / Reuters

4br, 41tl; China Newsphoto / Reuters 27c; China Photos / Reuters 57tl; Christie's Images 55cr; Claro Cortes IV / Reuters 44c; Justin Guariglia 28tr; Robert Harding World Imagery 21br; So Hing-Keung 44tr, 56-57b; Wolfgang Kaehler 9tl; Earl & Nazima Kowall 22tl; Reinhard Krause / Reuters 55tl; Simon Kwong / Reuters 58c, 69tr; Liu Liqun 23bc, 40bl, 49tr; Craig Lovell 37cr; James Marshall 6cl; Wally McNamee 69tl; Gideon Mendel 22b, 28b; Zeng Nian 57tr; Kazuyoshi Nomachi 26tr, 45tl; Reuters 35cr; Reuters / Guang Niu 17tr; Reuters / Kin Cheung 18tr; Reza / Webistan 17tl; Galen Rowell 63tl; Gilles Sabrie 20tl; Bob Sacha 3, 6bl; Bob Sasha 23clb; Michel Setboun 26bc; Keren Su 8bl, 20b, 32bl, 33bl, 62tr; Peter Turnley 16cl, 26clb; Julia Waterlow / Eye Ubiquitous 26cla; David H. Wells 32tl; Michael S. Yamashita 8tl, 13tl, 29cr, 34-35b; Bobby Yip / Reuters 17br; Zefa / Angelo Cavalli 24b; **DK Images:** Alan Hills / The British Museum 15tl; Chas Howson / The British Museum 71cr; Dave King / Courtesy of The Science Museum, London 50bc; Dave King / Courtesy of the University Museum of Archaeology and Anthropology, Cambridge 10tl; Judith Miller / Ancient Art 66cl; Judith Miller / Sloan's 10c, 18cl; Judith Miller / Sloans & Kenyon 66tr; Courtesy of the National Maritime Museum, London 50bl; Courtesy of the Pitt Rivers Museum, University of Oxford 11tl; Laurence Pordes / Courtesy of The British Library 15tl

(Inkstone); Karen Trist / Rough Guides 58cl; Alex Wilson / Courtesy of the Charlestown Shipwreck and Heritage Center, Cornwall 34cr (Tobacco); **Yanling Duan:** 14bc, 53tl; **Empics Ltd:** AP Photos / Greg Baker 29cr; **Getty Images:** 56clb; AFP 45tr, 51l, 69c; AFP / Liu Jin 29tl; AFP Photo / Frederic J. Brown 53bl; AFP Photo / Peter Parks 43br; Archive Photos 59c; Asia Images / Gareth Jones 16bl; Aurora / Ashley Gilbertson 15tr; Torsten Blackwood / AFP 57cr; Bongarts / Christian Fischer 60bl; Frederic J. Brown / AFP 38tr, 48tl; Clive Brunskill 60bc; China Photos 25tl; Cancan Chu 51tr; Fred Dufour / AFP 54-55b; Nir Elias / AFP 67br; Hulton Archive 67cla; The Image Bank / Keren Su 6tr; The Image Bank / Richard A. Brooks 44-45b; Liu Jin / AFP 7br, 55tr; David Levenson 68tr; Liaison / Paula Bronstein 53tr; Dylan Martinez / AFP 51br; Michel Porro 15b; Peter Rogers 33br; Stephen Shaver / AFP 63tr; Stone / Robert Van Der Hilst 25cr; Stone / Shuan Egan 31br; STR / AFP 56tr; Henri Szwarc / Bongarts 69br; Taxi / Keren Su 18bl, 42tl; Mark Thompson 61tl; **Ben Hoare:** 4tr, 23tl, 23ca, 23tr, 48cr; **The Kobal Collection:** Columbia / Sony / Chuen, Chan Kam 58cca; **Panos Pictures:** Natalie Behring 52b; D.J. Clark 47tl, 47br; Qilai Shen 21tr, 29tr; Chris Stowers 7tr; Gangfeng Wang 7cr; **Rex Features:** Everett Collection 59tl; Patrick Frilet 31tr; Richard Jones 58br; Lou Linwei 51cra; Peter Lou / Sinopix 49tl; Sipa Press

24tl, 29br, 35tr, 43bl; **The Ronald Grant Archive:** 58tl; **Still Pictures:** BIOS Gunther Michel 37br; BIOS Klein & Hubert 31c; Ecopix / Ullstein 25cl; Russell Gordon 41tr, 46-47b; Hiss / Ullstein 25b; Thomas Roetting 14c, 19bl; ullstein - phalanx Fotoagentur 48cl; ullstein / Vision Photos 21tl; UNEP 46bl; **The Wellcome Institute Library, London:** 52tl.

Wall chart: Alamy Images: nagelstock.com (Great Wall); rochaphoto (One Child Poster); Keren Su / China Span (Panda); WorldFoto (Maglev). **Corbis:** Justin Guariglia (Docks); So Hing-Keung (Dragon Dance). **DK Images:** Courtesy of The British Library, London (Ink Stone); The British Museum, London (Calligraphy Brush); Judith Miller / Sloan's (Ming Vase); Courtesy of The Science Museum, London (Gunpowder). **Getty Images:** AFP (Shenzhou V); Michel Porro (Calligrapher). **Rex Features:** Sipa Press (Olympic Stadium). **Still Pictures:** Russell Gordon (Child on Computer).

Jacket: Front: Corbis: Alfred Ko cla; Bob Sacha cl; **Getty Images:** tr; Gavin Hellier **OnAsia:** Paul Harris tl. **Back: Alamy Images:** Comstock Images clb; **Corbis** tl; **Getty Images:** Image Bank b; **OnAsia:** Natalie Behring cr; John Lander tr

All other images © Dorling Kindersley
For further information see:
www.dkimages.com

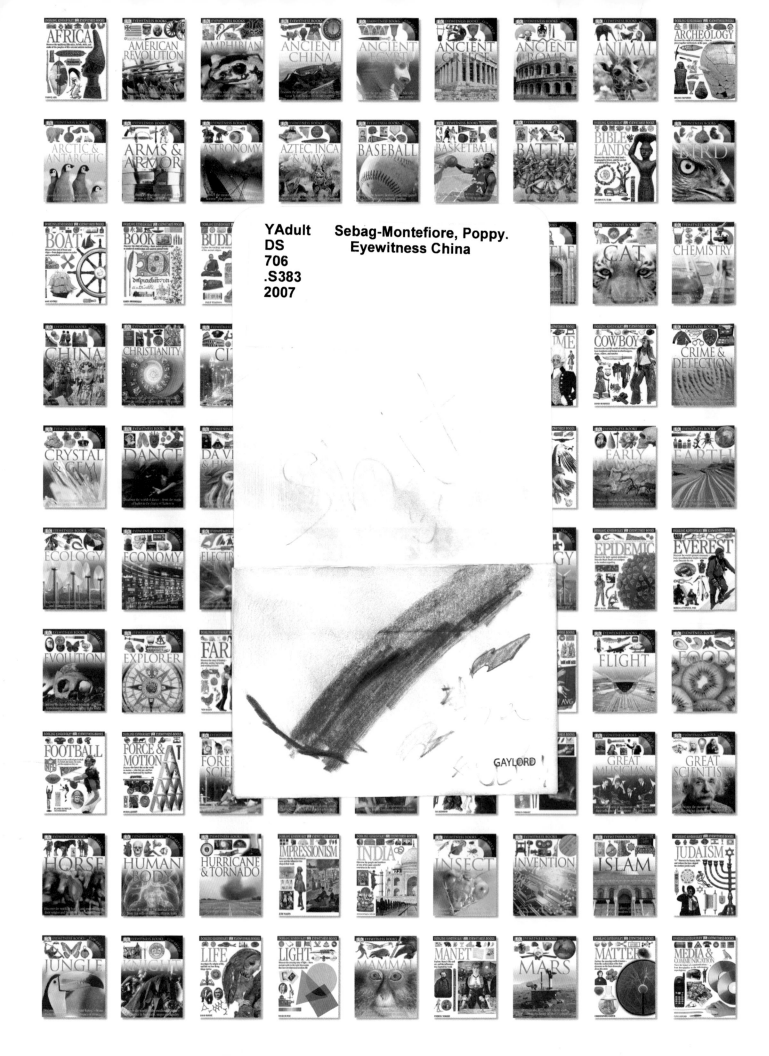